Annabel

READING AND RESPONSE

Edited by R. P. Hewett

A CHOICE OF POETS

A FURTHER CHOICE OF POETS

A CHOICE OF DRAMATIC THEMES

(Harrap's New Outlook Series)

READING AND RESPONSE

An Approach to the Criticism of Literature

BY

R. P. HEWETT

HARRAP LONDON

First published in Great Britain 1960
by HARRAP LIMITED
19–23 Ludgate Hill, London EC4M 7PD

Reprinted: 1962; 1963; 1967; 1969; 1973; 1975;
1977; 1979; 1982

ISBN 0 245-52757-5

Printed in Great Britain by
Mackays of Chatham Ltd

PREFACE

THIS book has been written in the hope that it may be helpful to students who are beginning to move beyond the early stages of 'reading for the story' and to enquire more deeply into the quality of their reading matter. It aims to bridge the often formidable gap between 'O' level work in English Literature and the much more demanding work at 'A' and 'S' levels. In recent years, too, examination and university authorities have more and more required from candidates—wisely, in my view—some capacity to read and evaluate texts they have not studied, and this book tries to offer help in developing such a capacity. It may also be of use to those fortunate sixth-formers who are not haunted by public examinations, but are pursuing a 'general course,' and to adult students concerned with literature at extra-mural classes.

The plan of the book is simple. Part One is largely discursive; it tries to start with the position in which the new sixth-former finds himself, and raises some of the important questions about reading practices and kinds of reading material. The first two chapters are each followed by some questions, related to the subject matter, which suggest further activity, and Part One concludes with a 'bridge' chapter which aims at showing in slow motion the process of close reading. Part Two gives some examples of critical readings under three headings: poetry, drama, and prose. Part Three offers further selections under the same three headings, each with 'leading' questions to the student, and finishes with a sample comparison between two poems and some related passages for the student himself to compare. The book concludes with two appendices which suggest some further reading.

I have nowhere aimed at any kind of completeness or 'coverage,' either literary or historical. I have purposely not put the passages in date order, partly to emphasize that the choices of material are personal, and partly to avoid even the appearance of claiming to offer anything complete. There is a great deal in Part One and no doubt also in the detailed commentaries which teachers and students may wish to quarrel with; my intention throughout has been to raise issues and promote discussion rather than lay down the law. The last thing I wish is that this book should be thought of as a guide or compendium.

I should like to thank my wife very warmly for listening to this material *seriatim*, for constant help and encouragement and for typing the manuscript, and my colleagues and publishers for advice and help.

R. P. Hewett

Trimley-St-Martin
Suffolk

ACKNOWLEDGMENTS

For permission to use copyright material the author is grateful to:

Messrs Edward Arnold, Ltd, and the author, for an extract from *A Passage to India*, by E. M. Forster.

Messrs Cassell and Co., Ltd, and the author, for "Lollocks," by Robert Graves, from *Collected Poems* 1959.

Messrs Chatto and Windus, Ltd, for "Anthem for Doomed Youth," by Wilfred Owen.

Messrs J. M. Dent and Sons, Ltd, for an extract from *The Heart of Darkness*, by Joseph Conrad.

Messrs Faber and Faber, Ltd, and the author, for an extract from *Murder in the Cathedral*, by T. S. Eliot.

Mr David Holbrook, for an extract from *English in the World To-day*.

Messrs William Heinemann, Ltd, and the Estate of the late Mrs Frieda Lawrence, for "Mosquito" and an extract from *Women in Love*, by D. H. Lawrence.

Messrs John Lane, the Bodley Head, Ltd, for an extract from *Ulysses*, by James Joyce.

Messrs Macmillan and Co., Ltd, and the Trustees of the Hardy Estate, for "During Wind and Rain" and an extract from *Tess of the d'Urbervilles*, by Thomas Hardy.

Messrs Sidgwick and Jackson, Ltd, for "The Soldier," by Rupert Brooke.

The Society of Authors, and the Public Trustees, for an extract from *St Joan*, by Bernard Shaw.

Mrs Thomas, for *Adlestrop* and *The Owl*, by Edward Thomas.

Mr Leonard Woolf, for an extract from *The Waves*, by Virginia Woolf.

Messrs A. P. Watt and Son and the Executors of the Estate of the late H. G. Wells, for an extract from *The History of Mr Polly*, by H. G. Wells.

CONTENTS

PAGE

Part One: READING IN GENERAL 13

Chap. 1. The Point of Reading 14

Chap. 2. Kinds of Reading 30

Chap. 3. The Reading Process in Slow Motion 61

i. Edward Thomas: *Adlestrop*
ii. Andrew Marvell: *The Garden*

Part Two: EXAMPLES OF CLOSE READING 75

Chap. 4. Some Poems Examined 76

i. William Shakespeare: *Sonnet 66*
ii. Edward Thomas: *The Owl*
iii. Anonymous: *O Waly Waly*
iv. William Blake: *London*
v. Thomas Hardy: *During Wind and Rain*
vi. Alexander Pope: from *Moral Essays*
vii. Gerard Manley Hopkins: *The Starlight Night*
viii. John Keats: *Ode to Autumn*

Chap. 5. Some Passages from Drama Examined 102

i. from *A Midsummer Night's Dream*
ii. from *Henry IV Part II*
iii. from *Macbeth*
iv. from *Antony and Cleopatra*
v. from *The Winter's Tale*

Chap. 6. Some Prose Passages Examined 128

i. D. H. Lawrence: from *Women in Love*
ii. Jonathan Swift: from *A Modest Proposal*
iii. Charles Dickens: from *Hard Times*
iv. James Joyce: from *Ulysses*
v. E. M. Forster: from *A Passage to India*
vi. Jane Austen: from *Mansfield Park*

Part Three: WORK FOR THE STUDENT 173

Chap. 7. Some Poems for Close Reading 174

i. Anonymous: *A Lyke-Wake Dirge*
ii. William Shakespeare: *O Mistress Mine*
iii. Geoffrey Chaucer: from *The Prologue to the Canterbury Tales*
iv. D. H. Lawrence: *The Mosquito*
v. Robert Graves: *Lollocks*
vi. Matthew Arnold: *To Marguerite (II)*
vii. John Donne: *The Sun Rising*

Chap. 8. Some Dramatic Passages for Close Reading 194

i. Shakespeare: from *Henry V*
ii. Shakespeare: from *Much Ado About Nothing*
iii. Shakespeare: from *Hamlet*
iv. Shakespeare: from *Julius Cæsar*
v. Shakespeare: from *Othello*
vi. G. B. Shaw: from *Saint Joan*
vii. T. S. Eliot: from *Murder in the Cathedral*

Chap. 9. SOME PROSE PASSAGES FOR CLOSE READING 210

i. Clarendon: from *History of the Great Rebellion*
ii. Thomas Hardy: from *Tess of the D'Urbervilles*
iii. Samuel Butler: from the essay *Quis Desiderio . . .?*
iv. Francis Bacon: from the essay *Of Travel*
v. Henry Fielding: from *Tom Jones*
vi. Joseph Conrad: from *The Heart of Darkness*

Chap. 10. SOME PASSAGES FOR COMPARISON 228

Introduction and Worked Example:

(*a*) Rupert Brooke: *The Soldier*
(*b*) Wilfred Owen: *Anthem for Doomed Youth*

i. (*a*) Thomas Campion: *Vivamus mea Lesbia atque amemus*
(*b*) Ben Jonson: *Vivamus mea Lesbia atque amemus*

ii. (*a*) Sir William Temple: from an essay, *Moor Park Garden*
(*b*) George Eliot: from *Adam Bede*

iii. (*a*) William Wordsworth: *She dwelt among th'untrodden ways*
(*b*) Hartley Coleridge: *He lived among th'untrodden ways*

iv. (*a*) Robert Herrick: *To Daffodils*
(*b*) George Herbert: *Life*

v. (*a*) Virginia Woolf: from *The Waves*
(*b*) H. G. Wells: from *The History of Mr Polly*

vi. (*a*) Ben Jonson: from *Volpone*
(*b*) William Congreve: from *The Way of the World*

APPENDICES

A. A List of Suggestions for Further Reading 251
B. Some Critical and Related Books 253

Part One

READING IN GENERAL

Chapter One

THE POINT OF READING

In the past twenty years or so reading as a practice and art has tended to diminish—at any rate the reading of imaginative work for the satisfactions it offers to the imagination. It is, therefore, perhaps worth restating the functions and purposes of reading, and insisting on its indispensability. Even a superficial glance at the development of a child can show how much he gains from the reading process—in knowledge, in range, and, perhaps more important, in a series of interior satisfactions and fulfilments which cannot at present be gained any other way. This is one of the reasons why education, or rather literacy, is equated with the capacity to read.

WHY WE READ

Reading brings us, potentially, the whole world except for that tiny segment of it which we can experience directly. Our direct experiences are limited by our total social circumstances—where and how we live, what money and facilities we have—and ultimately by the fact that we must die. The range of experience available to us through reading is unlimited; but it is not merely a question of quantity. The most important kinds of reading are those which in some way affect the segment of life that is within the range of our direct experience, by increasing our understanding of ourselves and others, improving our powers to discriminate, and thus enriching the quality of our lives. From this it follows that the most rewarding kinds of reading are not merely those which offer information (knowledge about things), important though this may be, or entertainment (interest without relevance), though this too can play its part, but the body of *imaginative* writing, which deals with the attitudes, feelings, responses to experience, and aspirations of man in general, and is therefore necessarily relevant to our own experiences. What are rather drearily called the classics, or 'serious' literature, are in fact the best of those pieces of writing, whether poetry, prose, or drama, which claim to make, implicitly or explicitly, statements about 'Life' in general—and therefore about us. To be able to discriminate in this field between the false and the true, between glitter and glow, between the superficial and the fundamental, is of quite unusual value. This capacity is called criticism, and all good reading will tend to develop a critical capacity, a tool of increasing precision. The object of this book is not to analyse the critical process, but to suggest some means of close reading which may develop the faculty in the individual student, and to stimulate in him (or her) the true interior delight in imaginative reading. This final product, the object of the whole process, is something that cannot be taught directly: but if this book encourages the discovery or development of the power in the reader it will amply have fulfilled its rôle.

First, though, we must learn *how* to read. We are surrounded on all sides by print, most of it expendable, as in newspapers and periodicals, much of it grossly motivated, as in advertising, and a good deal of it cut-price, reach-me-down, and repetitive as in the cheap novel. To find a path through this morass of material is difficult enough, for the impact of much of it is only half conscious. Just as the palate of a man may be so soaked in sauces and condiments that he can no longer react to the taste of good plain bread even though he might admit that it is the "Staff of Life," so the palates of many people are so blunted by too much titillation that they can no longer distinguish between a passage of lush prose advertising bottled beer and a genuine poem. Their taste buds have atrophied. Only the most careful training while his taste is in the process of formation can save a child from this fate—so continuous is the flood of print. In the end his hard-won literacy—the power to read which so many undeveloped nations are making efforts to gain at whatever cost—enables him only to make tepid automatic responses to a mass of indiscriminate material: and he uses this precious power of reading only on the sports columns and comic strips of the daily newspaper, the weekly 'gossip' magazines, and the posters on the hoardings. In many houses to-day, and not only among the poorest sections of society, there are no full-length books whatever—because people have ceased to respond to anything longer than a paragraph.

The printed word haunts us, in fact, with its blandishments and insistence; and if we cannot discriminate, a dull acceptance, extremely and manifestly dangerous, particularly in the field of politics ("I saw it in the paper") is our only response; or, at a slightly more sophisticated level, we may develop a cynical feeling that it is all lies ("You can't believe a word you're told"). Total acceptance and total rejection are obviously equally undesirable.

COMPETITORS OF READING

The current status of reading is also endangered from other directions. The cinema, radio, and television all act as competitors, and the last two, at least, as substitutes for reading.

The relation between these media and reading is a very complex one, but it is not necessary to go into much detail to show the difference. Reading is done at one's own pace, not at a pace dictated by the medium; it is possible and indeed desirable to re-read, either the whole work or passage from it, at intervals decided by the reader and in accordance with his personal needs; he can read what he wants to when he wants to; the possible range of reading is infinite, and in comparison the possible range of, say, television is very restricted. Above all, he forms a series of images from the written word—images of far greater complexity and far more personal quality than he could expect to see on a screen. Reading is in fact an *activity*, in which the whole man is involved—eye and ear and imagination and memory—whereas the other media far too often require only *passivity*. Moreover it is a highly selective and personal activity, concerned with personal tastes and not determined by the tastes of millions of others. Good reading is a creative activity; and whatever merits can be allowed to viewing or listening to radio, cinema, and television, they are seldom indeed either active or creative.

The cinema is now certainly beginning to lose the struggle to occupy the major recreational time of people as against television: but during the thirties and early forties in this country it was used particularly by young people as an escape from their day-to-day world. For example, a fourteen-year-old girl in a London grammar school once told me that she went to five cinemas a week, and added with no trace of shame or feeling of loss that she "didn't read books." I discovered that she had not read a full-length book outside school since she was ten. This, one hopes, is an extreme example, and such addiction must be rare now; but it is a pointer.

The radio for many years was used in countless houses as a blanket to smother conversation or reading: when conversation was necessary one talked *through* the Light Programme or Radio Luxembourg, and this was perhaps a measure of how highly its outpourings were valued. But radio allowed one to indulge in some pursuit and even, occasionally, to read—if music of the kind one hears rather than listens to were being broadcast, or if one's ears were sufficiently habituated to a flow of sound for it to be ignored. Indeed, another pupil in the same grammar school, an able sixteen-year-old with rather poor home circumstances, told me that he found he couldn't work in the local library reading-room because it was too quiet for him to be able to concentrate.

A much more serious inroad into the practice of reading is, of course, made by television. More than four-fifths of the families in this country owned television sets by mid-1959, and their use in what may well be the only sitting-room in winter effectually prevents reading, because of the hypnotic screen and the continuous sound. Reading is inevitably 'squeezed out' in such a household. It has been calculated that the average person has a television addiction period of about five years—a serious loss of other activities even in the life of an adult, but crippling indeed if the victim is a child; one has only to think of the period between eight and thirteen or ten and fifteen. Children and young people easily form habit patterns, and television seems to fulfil all the needs of such patterns. It is easy and available —("Let's just see what's on," "We must see the so and so's")—it is widely publicized, and it provides a total dream world with a set of familiar personalities whom one 'knows' intimately. All these factors contribute to elbowing out other activities or interests, particularly among young people.

Of all the mass media affecting people to-day, television is having a greater competitive influence against the practice of reading than any other. This is not to suggest, however, that the problem would be solved if television (or *a fortiori* cinema or radio) had never been invented, still less that it is intrinsically worthless; on the contrary, it offers a potentially exciting new medium which is capable of producing most interesting work. The points that need making are, firstly, that it is used grossly and indiscriminately at present, and this, together with the unmistakeable fact that most programmes, like most films, are ephemeral or trifling, makes its total effect harmful; secondly, and far more important for my present purposes, that even if all television were imaginatively produced by really creative producers it would never and could never be a substitute for reading.

In summary, then, reading is the indispensable centre of the educational—the learning—process, and in the future, as far as one can foresee, will continue to be so. Many efforts have been made to put forward substitutes: 'visual aids' as they are used in some schools will serve as an illustration from the educational world, and illustrated 'strip' versions of children's classics from the world of commerce; but they all ignore this central necessity. Next to the personal experiences that constitute direct living, some of the deepest enrichments available in our society come from a full, varied and deep experience of the art of reading.

MODES OF READING

In a later chapter (Chapter 2) an attempt is made to analyse the main kinds of reading that are available, and to suggest methods of finding one's way about them. Here it is necessary to distinguish between various 'modes' of reading, and to show their applications.

A great deal of the reading matter we see in our daily life is by definition ephemeral. The material of newspapers and most, though not all, of the matter of periodicals is written to be discarded. To read an old newspaper found lining a drawer will show how little is left when it no longer retains its one virtue of topicality. It follows that one should develop a technique of quick discursive reading where the material is of the kind of which one needs only a summary—and it is one of the marks of an inexperienced reader that he reads everything at the same pace and with the same degree of attention. The capacity to extract what one wants from a newspaper is a fairly skilled one and a valuable one to acquire, and much of the careful plodding reading that newspapers are given is unnecessary, inappropriate to their own terms of reference, and wasteful of time. More dangerous, though, is the assumption that important work—the finest prose and poetry, for example—can be read with the off-hand technique that one has become used to with the daily reading of newspapers and periodicals. The finest pieces of writing will not yield their full meaning without concentration and scrutiny. The most extreme example of this kind of reading occurs when a major work of literature—say a mature play of Shakespeare at one end of the scale, or a simple and yet profound folk-song at the other—is read in childhood, constantly re-read throughout one's life, possibly almost learned by heart, and yet continues to yield more and more meaning and relevance. Contact with a work capable of this depth of 'reading' must necessarily be utterly different in kind from the first, probably the only, contact with a newspaper intended to light the fire next morning and to be completely forgotten in a week.

But the contrast between the 'consumable' newspaper and the inexhaustible poem is over-simplified. It has already been pointed out that we are surrounded on all sides by floods of reading matter, and one of the major problems for a person learning to read with discrimination is to find a way of 'keeping his head above water'—to learn, in fact, how to choose what is worth his real attention and what can be fairly quickly discarded. This will perhaps be made clearer if we look briefly at the literature produced for people younger than those who are assumed to be reading this book.

CHILDREN'S READING

At eleven or so many boys go through a phase of addiction to series of books with the same war hero as their leading character. To re-read them, even at sixteen or seventeen, is a chastening experience, still more to do so as an adult. We wonder how we could ever have enjoyed such crass and repetitive made-to-measure situations, such cardboard black-and-white characterization, such manifest sprinkling of the text with physical violence at regular intervals of so many pages, such poverty of imagination or originality, such threadbare dialogue, such reliance on the elementary mechanism of "what happens next?" We can, of course, simply shrug the whole matter off, and say that such tastes are juvenile and that we have outgrown them. But if we re-read, say, *Huckleberry Finn*, which we also may have liked at that stage or a little later, we find that it stands up admirably to our more mature sense of values and judgment. The criteria that we apply now are satisfied by the intrinsic qualities of the book: the people in it are real people, the situations are genuinely imagined and have the characteristic oddity and yet relevance of real life: a re-reading leaves us, not bored and incredulous and reflecting on how far we have travelled and developed since those early days, but simultaneously retaining or remembering the warm affection in which we held the book in the past, and aware that there are depths and richnesses in it which we could not then recognize but which we can now see. Such books 'work' for our (relatively) adult taste, and the experience seems to have been a valid one at eleven *because* it is valid now at seventeen. A similar experiment can be conducted in relation to one's reading at any age. Look again, for example, at the little books of Beatrix Potter and compare them with a current 'comic' for five-year-olds, or at *The Wind in the Willows* in relation to the works of Enid Blyton, or at the works of Arthur Ransome in relation to the 'William' books, and you will find that the first in each pair offers a certain fullness even now, and that the second is empty. The same test is more difficult to apply to your more recent reading, because you may still be partially addicted to books which later on you will consider trifling: but most readers at this stage will agree that to compare, say, *Moonfleet* with the current spate of glossy 'war-books' is to compel a similar judgment. Distinctions of a similar kind can be drawn between books intended for any age, and can be illustrated in detail by quotation and comparison.

The fact is that there has been in the last thirty years or so a formidable exploitation of what is typically called 'the juvenile market.' The process began with the first School Board Act of 1870, when elementary education was made compulsory for all children, and a vast new readership emerged. Up to the First World War the books intended especially for children showed a certain sense of responsibility—indeed, the fiction was often interspersed with crude 'tacked-on' moralizing, or made the vehicle of an unrealized religiosity; but between the two wars standards rapidly fell, until in the thirties and particularly since the last war, the *only* criterion seemed to be selling-power. The lowest point of this process, one hopes, was reached with the American so-called 'horror comics,' now fortunately banned in this country, but a great deal of other material was written for children that was harmful or at the least shoddy and unnourishing. Every reader of this book must remember the children's annuals, a few of which were not without value, but the bulk of which were meretricious pulp—the brightly coloured covers, the over-thick strawy paper, the poor grey print, the threadbare stories and scribbled illustrations, the wretched coy little 'poems,' all illustrating the assumption that "anything will do for children." There is a welcome trend now in the opposite direction, which began with an effort by publishers, writers, and artists to produce really worthy books for very young children, and there is now a good deal of responsible and imaginative writing for children up to the mid-teens; but there is still a vast amount of trash, poorly presented and without nourishment of any kind.

The adolescent is in many ways even worse off. The particular tastes he is assumed to have are shamelessly exploited. A continuous eroticism, thinly veiled sadism masquerading as frankness or reportage, an insistence that only the pettifogging and superficial in music, art, literature, or life in general, could ever interest "the average teen-ager" —this is the stock-in-trade of the bulk of cheap periodicals to-day. Most of those that offered something a little less trifling, whether for adolescents or adults, have been squeezed out of the market or forced into liquidation; a glance at a bookstall will show how true this is. Such magazines assume that, if the buyer can read at all, his reading stamina is strictly limited and his diet must be spiced with illustrations, presented in tabloid style ('snappy' is the journalist's word) and chopped up into tiny paragraphs, with the typography continually varied in an effort to induce the jaded attention of the reader, already saturated with such nagging insistences for years past. The assumption is that a page of uniform print is too much for the adolescent to manage.

The kind of periodical briefly described above is vaguely intended for 'the young reader,' though widely read by adults. Women's magazines deserve a special study of their own: it is worth noting, for example, how patronizing is the tone of some of them, how low the level of literacy they expect, and how wide is the general assumption that the woman reader is not much more than half-witted. But enough has been said to make the general point: and an appetite constantly stimulated (and yet never satisfied) by such ephemeral publications will find the solider diet of more valuable reading depressing or indigestible, much as a physical diet of predigested 'pap' or cheap sweets vitiates the taste for solid and nourishing food.

Full-length books have not been much discussed yet: a fuller treatment is given in Chapter 2. Here it is only necessary to say that cheap novels, ranging from the paper-covered love or crime story, which is frequently quite illiterate, to the ampler bulk of many 'best-sellers,' can be equally harmful in the way that they spoil the palate. Reading such books is often an almost hypnotic process, and to say of them that they are "intensely readable" or that "one can't put them down" is another way of suggesting that they are drugs. The "young reader" has indeed a hard task to form any standards at all when faced by this mass of worthless reading matter.

A DIGRESSION ON ADVERTISING

Advertisements, which add to the mass of half-absorbed print, cannot be given an extended treatment here; but they repay analysis, and the analytical process itself helps to produce some immunity to their worst effects. This is not to suggest that there are not honest, informative, and modest advertisements: but most popular advertising appeals, with varying degrees of subtlety, to one's ignorance (pseudo-scientific advertisements complete with doctors holding stethoscopes, or scientists with test tubes in laboratories), one's snobbery (you can't afford to be without so-and-so, the best people use this-or-that), one's envy (keeping up with the Joneses) or one's fears ("Are you doing the best you can for your child?" "Is your shape or your smell or your clothing offensive or unfashionable or ugly?"). This constant nagging by advertisements has many important sociological results, with which we are not directly concerned here, but also contributes to the devaluation of language. Every time a string of superlatives appears in an advertisement cynically puffing some product, they lose some of their validity, and a process occurs rather like the devaluation of coinage, until in the end the words lose all their original significance and deteriorate into meaningless symbols. If every film in every cinema every week is "arresting," "world-shaking," "stupendous," or even quite simply "the greatest in the world," what words are we left with to describe, say, a real event of great splendour, or a really major work of art? To be insulated against these transparently venal appeals is of great value in being able to read, and indeed to feel, properly in one's own right.

Discrimination, then, which is the quality that this book aims at stimulating and bringing out, has a hard time of it in the current situation. Much of what the young person reads involuntarily, on hoardings for example, consists of flat lies; most of the periodicals he sees are flashily presented puerilities, sometimes poison, and the great bulk of published books are, to put it no higher, worthless in the sense defined at the beginning of this chapter—unable, that is, to add anything beneficial to one's personality or understanding. It is not surprising that most adolescents' tastes in literature (when they read at all) are so appalling: what *is* surprising is that so many still have any power to discriminate at all, so battering is the cataract of words. We ought therefore to be quite sure of the positive advantages of reading selectively, or we may indeed resign ourselves to the belief that the task is hopeless.

THE REWARDS OF READING

What, then, can we get from a power to read with discrimination? The products are very difficult to discuss or even define, because what one is aiming at is not accessible directly to the teacher or to the student. To put it in another way, just as swimming can be taught but pleasure in swimming cannot, so the pleasure of reading—a quality quite distinct from superficial 'entertainment'—is itself 'unteachable,' and unrecognizable by the student until he has acquired it. The process of learning to read well is not at all like the acquisition of a definite body of knowledge (though this will often help), but is the far trickier, more elusive, and more essential process of 'learning to like' something. And this product—the pleasurable emotions that derive from something fine properly read and grasped—is not merely a marginal accompaniment of the process of reading, but the very essence of it. The acid test is the 'true interior delight' mentioned at the beginning of this chapter—a delight in complete contrast with the admiration for great literature that students are still taught to pretend, even where there is no trace of real response. The solid blocks of literary history that are offered by teachers and textbooks are no substitute for this delight, useful though they may be in regulating and relating a series of personal responses. It is very difficult to convince the unpersuaded that reading, real reading, is the source of some of the richest pleasures that life can offer, and all one can hope for is that the student will himself discover the authentic experience.

This full flower comes only when he is beginning to read without instructions and to develop powers of his own.

Reading, then, is a personal experience, and the experience is authentic when it provides a genuine personal pleasure, the pleasure that comes from using one's whole personality in the process of perception and evaluation. Wordsworth said in a wonderful phrase that "nothing worth while was ever taught except through pleasure." This kind of pleasure has to be distinguished from the bored acquiescence that is often our only reading experience, or the standardized thrills to which we tend to respond as a machine does when we put a penny in the slot. It is a richer, deeper, more lasting, and more *relevant* experience than that.

I cannot do better in concluding this introduction than to quote the words of David Holbrook in an article on *English in the World To-day*:

> Not only is our written and spoken language inadequate for living with others . . . it cuts us off by its limited range and quality from our literature and 'the best that has been known and thought in the world.'
>
> So we are deprived of a main source of succour in ordinary living. The *hardest* things in the world are the quietest and the simplest: the organizing of one's being in the experience of love, in family life, choosing one's path in the use of one's talents, facing the betrayals inevitably brought by time and chance, coming to terms with the loss of friends by death, the extension of sympathy to others: these are the subjects of literature; they are the province of the organized word from the proverbial saying to such a great work as *The Winter's Tale*. The experience of these things in imaginative literature, where we follow those who walk ahead, can help us to achieve balance in thought and feeling. The quality of our individual capacities to be ourselves, to live spontaneously and fully in and through our large and small daily experiences, *is* civilization.

This admirable formulation is what we should keep in mind whenever the effort to read independently seems too great, whenever we find ourselves longing for the comforting solidity of 'mere' facts and begin to hate this vague flux of thought and feeling, whenever we find ourselves reverting to the easy satisfactions of cheap publications. The experience of independently enjoying real literature will offer, once it is established—and in the last analysis only the individual can establish it—a quality of the greatest value, which no "moving accident," none of the "shocks that flesh is heir to," can destroy.

Topics for discussion or further activity

1. Do you ever read your younger brothers' or sisters' books and periodicals? Can you discriminate between the good and the bad *for them*? How do you do it?

2. Write a short statement, to be read aloud, on why any given current periodical is popular. Make a case for or against such a periodical, to be discussed in class, and illustrate it by actual copies of the magazine and by extracts from it.

3. Choose the novel, or play, or poem, which you most often re-read, and say in some detail why.

4. Make a collection of cut-out advertisements which in your view appeal to the reader's fears, snobbery, envy, ignorance, greed. Find some advertisements which seem to you good and honest, and discuss them in class.

5. How much time do you spend on seeing or hearing radio, television, films? What in your own experience does reading offer that the other media don't, and vice-versa?

6. Instance a book which you once liked and which you now dislike (or vice-versa). Try to show what you once thought of it and what has caused the change in your feelings.

7. Make a list of the full-length books you have read in the past year and give them grade marks: A for excellent, B for good, C for average, and D for poor. Compare these with the grades given by other members of the class.

8. Compare a novel you have read with a film or television version of it that you have seen. What do you think was gained in the change of medium, and what lost?

Chapter Two

KINDS OF READING

THIS chapter will consider the current 'reading situation,' and try to draw distinctions between various classes of reading matter. It is not possible to deal with these questions in detail or definitively in this confined space; many of the subjects dealt with here in a single paragraph deserve, and have had, full-length books to themselves. The most that one can hope for is to encourage the student to stand back a little from his own reading context and examine it, and to provide some topics for further consideration or discussion.

THE READING SITUATION

The general statement has already been made that the printed material we are offered to-day is largely ephemeral; we need now to look rather more closely at this statement. A great deal of our reading matter is either more vulgarized or more specialized than ever before: vulgarized in the sense that many of the novels, plays, essays, are inherently inferior to many which have gone before, specialized in the sense that there is a vast output of highly technical writing, much of it very good, but written for a particular audience and often with narrow aims and intentions. With the second category we are not now particularly concerned, though mention is made of it later; the distinctions we wish to draw are in the first category—what can broadly be called imaginative, or at least pseudo-imaginative, writing. What do people actually read in this field now?

To look at the mass-circulation libraries may provide a

lead here. The public libraries in every town offer a very wide range of reading material: they are products of the last eighty years or so, and show in their history and attitude the characteristics of the period of mass literacy which brought them into being. The original assumption behind the provision of these libraries was that mass literacy would inevitably cause an increasing appetite for 'serious' literature, and this is reflected by the practice in some libraries of issuing two kinds of borrower's tickets—the 'general' ticket, on which one may borrow fiction or other books, and the 'non-fiction' ticket, on which one may not borrow novels. Fiction is thus still frowned on mildly—at least a diet of fiction only is quietly disapproved by this system. This attitude goes back to the days when young ladies secretly read novels hidden behind philosophical or theological works; there are amusing references to this attitude in Jane Austen's *Northanger Abbey*. Mid-Victorian children of the middle class were often forbidden to read fiction on Sundays, and this reflected the idea that the reading of novels is a sort of self-indulgence. One would think that by now fiction would be recognized as a major branch of imaginative writing, and there is something charmingly old-fashioned in the library committee's distinction; yet when we look at the bulk of material on the fiction shelves we can see their point. But it would be wrong to imagine that the non-fiction actually read is necessarily any better. Public libraries publish annual reports of the use made of their books, and print analyses of the number of books borrowed under various headings—philosophy, travel, biography, fine and applied arts, and so forth. The vast majority of books read are always fiction, but substantial numbers of non-fiction books are also read. These include a large number of useful but strictly informative books on technical matters, gardening, house design, 'how to do it,' sport; then there is travel, biography, 'juvenile,' and so forth. Probably only a relative handful of borrowers are serious readers of poetry, drama, criticism—the things with which we are particularly concerned; and just as good fiction, which is bound to be fairly rare, is read by very few readers, so the label 'non-fiction' is not in itself a guarantee of seriousness or quality. The *contents* of the library are often no index of what is borrowed: and since the books are acquired by municipal authorities there is a fair amount of high-mindedness, sometimes ill-informed, in their choice. Nevertheless public libraries do, of course, an enormous amount of good, and offer an indispensable source of material for all serious readers.

The subscription libraries which used to be attached to multiple chemists or booksellers give a clearer picture of what was actually being read, at any rate by the middle-class people who formed their main *clientèle*. Here the process was purely commercial, and the choice determined by demand. Several of these libraries had their books divided under headings such as the following: General Fiction, Light Romance, Thrillers, Westerns, and Non-Fiction—the last about a quarter of the whole. The General Fiction section contained most of the new fiction published in this country, and the books were bought in bulk as they appeared. After a year or so they were withdrawn, first to sections available to subscribers who paid a lower rate, and then, within a couple of years at the most, to special bookshelves where they were offered as remainders at a few pence; and they finished as a 'job-lot'. The main criterion here was certainly one of topicality: only recently published books were wanted, and you would generally search in vain for any of the classics of fiction. 'Light Romance' was an extraordinary section on its own, of fiction that doesn't make any claim to be literature, and was written 'for the market' on strictly commercial lines: "light" appeared to mean that the books should not be taken seriously, and "romance" meant generally that they were concerned with love, but in an unrealistic way. This type of book is still in demand and the category 'romance' appears regularly in some paper-back catalogues. "Thrillers" are still listed, then consist either of straight detective stories, in which the point is to spot the criminal, generally a murderer, before the revelation is made, or books which describe some desperate situation, often within a set of regulations almost as formal as the movements of a ballet. "Westerns," too, survive surprisingly in urban England, and their main characteristic is that the whites are very white, the blacks very black, and every one is quick on the draw or handy with his fists. These three fiction sub-varieties are marked by being very much cut to pattern, written to order within rigid conventions of ritualistic force; the result is that any one is very much like any other. A few writers of ability may have concerned themselves with detective stories or thrillers, but it is safe to say that writers of Light Romance or Westerns, as well as most thriller-writers, are strictly venal; they write with their tongues in their cheeks to satisfy the apparently unlimited demands of readers who want "the same again."

The 'non-fiction' sections of some paper-back displays are equally revealing. They are dominated by travel, biography, and reminiscence, mostly chatty and a great deal of it 'book-making.' What you will not find is any serious or scholarly work to speak of (unless it has had a *succès de scandale* like Boswell's *Journals*): and you will find virtually no poetry, drama, or criticism.

Lower down the social scale comes the 'tupenny library,' a smallish selection of books, often managed by a central agency and displayed in a tobacconist's or general stores. One feature is that the dust covers are preserved by being stuck over with plastic material, which seems surprising until one realizes that the books are chosen largely by their covers. All the books are works of fiction, and ninety per cent. are light romances or thrillers. Often side by side with these rather pathetic thumbed-over collections are paper-backed novels, which themselves can be categorized. They include genteel stories about nurses or air stewardesses, atrociously printed in double column pages on a characteristic strawy paper; war books, a leading group at present, very widely read by adolescents and recognizable by glossy covers showing camouflaged infantry in steel helmets pushing their way through jungle or warships in choppy seas picked out by searchlights and bursting with gunfire; and works of near-pornography with gangsters and floozies who conduct their lives in evening dress or nightgowns, written in a singular, choppy, 'sawn-off' style that aims at being tough, but quickly palls for a reader with even a modicum of literacy.

Then there are countless magazines, mainly for women, which offer fiction in the form of serials or short stories, and these too have a particular style and *ethos* of their own; these magazines are often confusingly referred to as 'books' by their readers. Still further down the scale are the picture-story magazines, some with a running text for those who can read a little, some with dialogue in 'balloons.'

The point is that all this is 'fiction,' and the young reader who is beginning to enquire seriously into what is worth reading in the field has to start by clearing away this lush undergrowth, which is parasitical on the real novel. The writing of fiction is only two hundred years old in this country, and it is likely if not inevitable that works of real genius are rare; and, as a corollary, that more excellent novels were written in the first hundred and ninety years than in the last ten, though this is difficult to remember when reviewers' columns and advertisements offer us a dozen or so assorted masterpieces every week. The impulse which leads some people away from reading fiction at all is quite understandable in this situation: but there would be a serious loss if one's distaste for the amount of rubbish offered made one reject the whole.

THE NOVEL

What, then, can we say about good novels? What makes a good novel, what do we get from a good novel, what, indeed *is* a novel, apart from 'a piece of prose describing people who are partly or wholly the product of a writer's imagination'—a definition which includes the immense mass of commercial fiction described above?

Here it is difficult, if not impossible, to generalize, because the *range* of good novels is itself very wide and does not submit itself to definition. Many attempts have been made to define a good novel and all of them can be shown to be inadequate by pointing out unquestionably fine novels which these definitions do not include. This has driven one critic to say that "a good novel is the kind of thing Jane Austen writes": and this is one way, however irritating, of meeting the problem. If one cannot define, one can at least exemplify: one can simply say that Jane Austen's *Emma* or Dickens' *Great Expectations* or Conrad's *Nostromo* or George Eliot's *Middlemarch* or D. H. Lawrence's *Sons and Lovers* are good novels. Novels are notoriously difficult to talk or write about in any coherent way. There has been remarkably little first-rate criticism of the novel, with one or two notable exceptions, some of which are mentioned in the appendix. One useful approach is to see what novelists themselves have to say about this art: D. H. Lawrence, for example, in his letters and literary criticism, though sometimes infuriating on the novel, is often very illuminating, and casts a great deal of light both on his own practice and on fiction in general. The opening chapter of each 'book' of Fielding's *Tom Jones* makes some interesting comments on his principles as a novelist. But such sources are rare, and many important novelists have seemed quite unable to discuss their own art coherently. Many of the difficulties are inherent in the form. It is partly a question of actual bulk: even the longest of Shakespeare's plays, *Hamlet*, is under four thousand lines in length; *Wuthering Heights*, which is much shorter than the average novel, runs to nearly twelve thousand lines in ordinary print. To hold any full-length novel in the mind, except as a "taste in the head," is difficult indeed.

Attempts have been made to deal with this difficulty by abstracting from the novel such elements as structure and character. Some interesting analytical work has been done on the *shape* of certain important novels, and this idea can sometimes be valuable: but too often one is left with the feeling that the subject-matter of the novel is somehow made irrelevant, and this produces absurdities. The examination of the *characters* of a novel seems more natural; indeed, it is the way most readers of novels judge what they read: but any good novel is more, much more, than the sum of its characters, and for novels of some kinds the analysis of character will be found to be restricting if not actually pointless. Moreover, characters tend to wilt when taken out of their natural element, the texture of the novel; one critic has said that the characters exist only in solution, but can be examined only as precipitates. Again, one can read novels as pictures of various periods, evoking the situations attitudes, people, and problems of a given time; this can be a very valuable approach, but clearly doesn't fully meet the problem, and may sometimes turn a living model into an antiquarian specimen.

We are driven to the conclusion that novels exist only in the actual context of their language: the final criterion of the quality of a novel, like that of any piece of writing, however short or long, is *the words on the page*. This is an idea which we are much preoccupied with in this book, and to keep it in mind will help us to avoid making too many loose generalizations, a pitfall to anyone who is trying to talk about novels.

A few generalizations must nevertheless be attempted, or the reader will feel completely at a loss. Most novels, for example, are about people, and we read them in order to discover more about people. The good novelist offers us an insight, belonging to a particular period or class or setting, into people—their relations, their aspirations, their hopes and fears. This is interesting because we like to know about 'others': but it is mainly important because of the light it casts on ourselves. We, too, are people: we have certain fundamental characteristics in common with all people—and more in common with the people imagined during the relatively recent literary form of the novel. The residual effect of a great novel is that it changes, in some degree, our perception of ourselves and our own 'setting.' The useful phrase "educating the emotions" is relevant here: all great literature, but particularly a great novel, because it shows people in action, *educates our emotions*, and leaves us to some degree changed by the experience of reading it.

Two digressions are now needed. One is concerned with 'contemporaneity.' If the impact on our own personalities and understanding is the important thing, does it not follow that the contemporary novel will be the most valuable, reflecting as it does current problems, current personalities, modern settings? This would perhaps be so if we could be sure of sorting out good novels from the incredible mixture we have already described: and indeed, contemporary novels should be read. Though I personally doubt that there have been many great novels written in the past ten years, this may be due to my ignorance of them, or to the mere fact that the sorting-out process takes time. Moreover, 'contemporary' denotes a short time compared with the last two hundred years, in which the sorting-out process has already been to some extent done. A reading course which did not grapple with fairly recent work would, I think, be a bad one, and a constant revaluation of the works of the past is necessary and essential. Nor should one take for granted or on trust the opinions of even the most eminent critics. The only test is in the reading, but there is no doubt that it is helpful to have some guidance, provided it is not dictatorial but merely suggestive. 'A classic'—to use a much-abused expression—is sometimes used to describe a book that has stood the test of time: but it is perhaps more useful to say that however much a picture of a past period is offered by a classic, it survives and has value only because it is not 'tied' to its setting, but deals with what is relatively permanent about human beings and is therefore relevant to us as it was to its contemporaries. Those novels which are *merely* contemporary, in fact 'modish,' die very quickly once the immediate situation they describe has changed, and for a novel to have an up-to-date setting or current dialogue is no guarantee that it will be really relevant to us.

The second digression concerns the 'historical' novel. This is a novel written about a different period from the one in which the writer lived: and on the whole—though there are a few notable exceptions—it is not as a form likely to attract the greatest novelists. It is characteristic of good novelists that they wish to deal with their own living situations, the actual flux of events in which they breathe. There seems something evasive in writing about the fourteenth century when living in the twentieth. Robert

Graves has written some interesting historical novels and they have often a very contemporary 'feeling': but his finest work by far, in my opinion, is his poetry, which is strictly contemporary in feeling and content. To take another example, the immense research which a fine novelist like George Eliot put into her solitary historical novel *Romola* produced, as most critics would agree, a monumental failure, with everything in it but life. A list of the dozen supremely great novels in English would not, I think, contain a single novel that was not contemporaneous in feeling and setting with its writer. The use of contemporary language, vital also to the poet, seems a necessary, though not sufficient, condition for a great novel.

The novel, then, introduces us to other modes of being than our own—other periods, other classes, other situations: and the informative and imaginative importance of this must not be underestimated. But its major rôle is to widen and deepen our own imaginative capacities. The greater the novel the more difficult it is to write about it, because the complete work is, as it were, a seamless garment. This becomes clear when one examines the abridged versions of novels that are often printed. It is probably not necessary to attack the illustrated 'strip' versions of classic novels here: their absurd inadequacy illustrates the belief that the greatness of a novel, its 'classicity,' lies solely in its story. Some abridgments of novels for schools are relatively successful, but the better the novel the more difficult generally it is to abridge it, and the worst treatment of all is to chop out sentences or phrases or single words and offer what is left in some such terms as "Every word written by Charles Dickens." The statement is true in fact but false in implication, because a good novel is a unity, and ranges from the unity of the whole work to the unity of the chapter, the paragraph, the sentence. All that is there—in a really good novel—is necessary. Even if you read a novel 'for the story' alone, the effect it has on you is the sum total of these localized experiences.

Good novels, nevertheless, can show their character 'in little' and in an extract, so long as it is not presented as a substitute for the book. It is the actual writing—the detailed handling of events, characters, symbols—that distinguishes the great writer from the others.

Elsewhere in this book some instances are given, on a necessarily limited scale, of this sort of judgment. But the final evaluation cannot be imposed from the outside; it can only come from the experience of reading the novels. The compiler or the critic may offer suggestions and stimuli, but he cannot, and should not try to, reproduce the experience itself. This is a general statement which applies to the whole process of detailed reading, and above all to the reading of a novel, where the total response is something too large to allow a verbal explanation except at a length similar to that of the novel itself. Nevertheless it must be insisted, first, that one can show *something* of the quality of a good novel by a short quotation from it, and secondly, that all good novels will submit themselves to some extent to this process. The characteristic tone of voice, range of interest and attitude, can be shown even in the short excerpt; and though it is no substitute whatever for the novel itself, it can form one mode of introduction to it.

Novels, especially modern ones, have only fairly recently been admitted to school syllabuses as 'set texts.' This is an admirable development. Students will be handicapped by the relative lack of a solid body of critical writing on the novel—compared at any rate with the vast amount that has been written on poetry and drama: but this, too, carries certain compensatory advantages, in that student and teacher will be forced to make their own judgments and not rely on those of the critics. It was really a somewhat grotesque situation at a time when nearly all the reading done voluntarily by adolescents was of fiction, that school and examination curricula should exclude any guidance in the one field where it was most needed.

When we move from fiction to the other two main kinds of imaginative writing—poetry and drama—we seem to enter a totally different world. Fiction is the dominant form of reading, as has been shown above, so we are moving in one sense into a very restricted world. There may be a very good poetry section in the local library, but it is seldom disturbed. The drama section may show an admirable range, but apart from an occasional student 'looking things up' or members of an amateur dramatic society searching for a play, it is likely to be very quiet. This is not difficult to test in practice or to illustrate by statistics, and a glance into a public library at peak periods will show how many people are looking for novels, especially those which have just been returned by other readers, and how few penetrate the vast echoing corridors of 'literature'—that is, in library classification, all imaginative writing except fiction.

POETRY

And yet from another point of view poetry is far *less* restricted than fiction. Poetry goes back to Homer; indeed as far back as we can trace any existence of imaginative language, poetry in some form seems to exist. There is some evidence that poetry originates in the *ictus* or beat that comes from various kinds of work-rhythms—pounding a mortar, paddling a boat, rocking a cradle. It seems to emerge with the dawn of community life of any kind. Thus its historical range is vast, its geographical range world-wide, its cultural range almost unlimited. It seems to have fulfilled some primordial need of human beings throughout nearly the whole of recorded history. Two hundred years ago most educated people read poetry as a natural and essential part of their lives, while the uneducated had a rich tradition of folk-song and folk-poetry, as well as the poetry of the Bible, to draw on. What is left of this now?

It is safe to say that only a relative handful of people now read poetry for pleasure—either the great works of the past or the poetry of their own contemporaries. Poetry is read in schools, and a few students take the taste for poetry with them into adult life. It is sometimes read on the radio. But for the rest it exists only in vestigial form—nursery rhymes, often bowdlerized or misunderstood, for very small children; 'lyrics' for dance music; the banal and somehow pathetic verses (about home or babies or love) that appear surrounded by little line drawings in odd corners of women's magazines, and the bits of 'poetic' prose or 'prose-poetry' which appear in the tabloid daily newspapers, and which reveal how deep-seated is the current distaste for poetry by being printed as prose though they rhyme at intervals.

To account for this almost complete drying up of the "springs of assent" in relation to poetry would take us very widely into educational, sociological, even philosophical realms, and is impossible here—though a mention of some of the possible factors involved is made at the end of this chapter. Here it is necessary to try to deal with one increasing attitude to poetry and to try to answer it. Any teacher will agree that a question more and more often asked, and with more and more weary disdain, is "What *use* is poetry? All that old-fashioned stuff!" Behind this is the feeling that even if poetry were at some period in the dim past really valued, it is no longer relevant to modern life. A more sophisticated version of the same idea is that poetry is primitive and diffuse, while modern people need concrete answers to concrete problems, which poetry, by definition, cannot supply. A crude answer to this sort of comment would be to point out that man is not an automaton, nor is he a walking brain: he has also a heart and feelings, which conflict with as well as complement his mind—and that poetry at its best resolves this conflict by speaking of and to the whole man, by stirring and satisfying him at some deeper level than the merely intellectual. The rhythmic elements in poetry, the chime of its rhymes, the oddity of its tone of voice, the way it echoes and yet rings the changes on speech rhythms—all these appeal simply and naturally to children: and if they don't appeal to adults it is not because they have outgrown the needs it fulfils, but because that side of their personalities has been blotted out and buried under the easier appeals of television, radio, cheap periodicals, and cheap fiction. Many adults thus find themselves not only unable to respond to any complexity in a piece of writing, but unable to respond even to the quiet emotional appeal of a folk-song or a ballad. They find it embarrassing to admit to having feelings apart from the crudest sentimentality (bunny-rabbits and babies) eroticism (pin-ups and smut), sensationalism (violence and accidents), or laughter. T. S. Eliot says in one of the *Preludes*:

> I am moved by fancies that are curled
> Around these images, and cling:
> The notion of some infinitely gentle
> Infinitely suffering thing.
>
> *Wipe your hand across your mouth, and laugh.*

The last line expresses the response of many people to an appeal to any but the crudest emotion. The capacity to respond is blunted and the only outcome is a snigger.

This is a very strange decline from the past when one considers the richness of English poetry. There is perhaps no literature in the world which has quite such a wealth of poetry. From the medieval anonymous poems onwards it is a parade of excellence—the most varied and the most profound to be seen in any country. For modern Englishmen to be quite so indifferent to poetry is a little like the Russians being indifferent to ballet, the Italians to painting, the Germans to music: the one field in which we are incomparably great is the one in which we show the greatest indifference. In the eighteenth century Pope made £8,000 from his verse translations of the *Iliad*: but no one to-day would dream of trying to live, even alone in a garret, on the monetary rewards of writing poetry.

The English poetic tradition was by no means limited to a highly educated minority. The common people had their own, which ran parallel to that of learned circles and constantly 'fertilized' it: ballads, folk-poetry, broadsheets, many of them sung as well as recited by single speakers or chorally. This tradition has only recently died; indeed, there are still remnants in some outlying parts of the British Isles and in the Dominions.[1] There is little hope of keeping it alive artificially, since an imposed tradition is a self-contradiction: but one can hope that a minority, perhaps through the schools, can keep alive an inclination to read and value poetry. It seems likely that the tradition has been squeezed out by the various social changes of the last sixty years; and of these changes, themselves immensely complex, the one that seems to need emphasizing here is the cultural one. Reading in general, and the reading of poetry in particular, tends to be a quiet activity and an individual one. Mr Richard Hoggart, having described the kinds of appeal made by cheap literature and periodicals, writes: "It is hard

[1] Two books which illustrate splendidly the range of this anonymous popular poetry are *The Common Muse*, *ed.* V. de Sola Pinto, and *The Idiom of the People*, *ed.* James Reeves.

to find a way through such a crowd, especially as the entertainers are adept at discouraging the subversive thought that outside there may be other, quieter regions."[1] The quieter regions of poetry are worth knowing about and visiting.

There have been hundreds of attempts to define poetry, like Johnson's "just representations of general nature," Wordsworth's "spontaneous overflow of powerful feelings,' Coleridge's "the *best* words in the best order," Michael Roberts' "an exploration of the possibilities of language." No attempt will be made to define it here, but it can perhaps be described obliquely. Poetry is a *heightened* language, which offers revelation rather than exposition, interpretation rather than statement. It does not so much demonstrate as extend the significance of what we may already 'know.' It is an expression of the whole man, and reveals what it is to be a whole man. It deals with the commonest issues of our lives and what is common to us all—love, nature, death. It can really no more be shrugged off than can life itself. If we allow to be blunted or destroyed the sense of wonder and delight that children show before they become self-conscious, before

> . . . shades of the prison house begin to close
> About the growing boy

we suffer a disabling loss.

> For our sense of wonder is not aroused by enormous, sensational things—though that is what a dulled sensibility requires to provoke it to a sort of *ersatz* experience of wonder.[2]

[1] *The Uses of Literacy*, p. 145.

[2] Josef Pieper, *Leisure the Basis of Culture* (quoted in *op. cit.* p. 192).

The modern distaste for poetry is partly caused by the kinds of poetry anthologized for schools. School anthologies are fast improving in range and content, but have tended till recently to be overweighted with poems from the nineteenth century, a period when an artificial 'poeticized' language was widely used, in an attempt to escape from the ugliness of contemporary industrial society. Quite young readers detect the falsity of such language. The pseudo-medieval mannerisms of, say, Tennyson's *Idylls of the King* must have done a good deal to confirm this dislike. Even anthologies which claimed to be 'modern' were often heavily coloured by this sort of writing: if the Tennyson so often anthologized is watered-down Keats, then the poetry of some of the Georgians was watered-down Tennyson. This tradition dies hard; school stock cupboards have still plenty of such material. We cannot limit the school reading of poetry to contemporary poems (though we could at least make sure that the modern poems read are not in this faded tradition), but we can at least avoid those poems, whether modern or not, which use a diction and tone remote from their period. Wordsworth said that poetry should be written in "a selection of the language of real men," and though this statement raises many difficulties, it is a useful test. The greatest poets write in a selection of the language of their own times, and one can regard with suspicion any poet who adopts the mannerisms and vocabulary of the past as a general practice. Just as the best novels are contemporary with their writers, so are the best poems: they come from a living situation and inevitably are expressed in the living language of the time.

An essential aspect of experiencing poetry which has already been touched on, and is emphasized in the examples and exercises that follow, perhaps ought also to be mentioned here. The impact of poetry, about which it is so difficult to generalize, consists of sound *and* sense. Poetry has not been read until it has been read aloud.[1] An analogy with music comes to mind, perhaps a dangerous one and certainly not one that should be pressed too far: but the reading of poetry aloud *is* rather like the performance of music. The music exists in potential form in the score, but is not *realized* until it is played instrumentally; and poetry too needs the direct impact of its sound and rhythm on the ear as well as the intellectual appreciation of this sound that one gets by reading visually. But the word 'performance' should not be taken too literally: a good deal of public reading of poetry, especially on the radio, is 'performed' in the bad sense; that is, it is declaimed in a histrionic way by professional actors, who may produce a beautiful sound which is yet unrelated to the poem. The best readers have a kind of neutrality of voice which the poem itself 'speaks through.' This is a difficult art; it is possible to cultivate, but has little in common with 'elocution' as usually understood; and a skilled use of the voice and tone is useless unless it is preceded by a thorough study and grasp of the poem.

Of the many kinds of poetry—lyrical, epic, dramatic, narrative, elegaic, satirical—the lyrical poem is probably the earliest form, the most universal in appeal, and the best point at which to start the study, and the enjoyment, of poetry. For this reason most of the poems chosen for close reading later in this book are lyrics of one kind or another. The history, the interconnexions and interdependences of English poetry make a vast study of their own: but they cannot precede or replace the individual experience of the single unique poem. Again, we are reduced to saying that although we cannot define poetry we can say with

[1] There is a great deal to be said for reading novels, or parts of novels, aloud—though life is too short for much of this; and drama needs performing as well as reading; but for poetry this reading aloud is essential in a much more fundamental way.

reasonable assurance that this, and this, and this, are poems. Nor can we *make* anyone enjoy poetry: we can only try to demonstrate how it *can* be enjoyed and stimulate the reader to do so for himself. The pervasive indifference to poetry is, as has been suggested, due to factors which we can to some extent fight against, and it is the last few decades which are 'out of step' with the whole of the rest of history. If almost totally illiterate peasants can produce and enjoy poetry of the quality of *O Waly Waly* or the *Lyke-Wake Dirge* (see pp. 82 and 174), there is nothing inherent in the modern far more 'educated' student to prevent him from at least an equal appreciation. The enjoyment of poetry is not something that can be faked, and patience and open-mindedness are indeed necessary; but learning is not in itself essential, and however dull and academic 'the study of poetry' may sound, it is a potential source of the greatest delight, excitement, and satisfaction.

DRAMA

Drama as a literary form raises many problems of its own, chief of which is perhaps the question whether it *is* a literary form, or something different in kind from poetry and fiction, both of which are meant to be read. The common-sense view seems to be that drama, as it was written to be acted, should be regarded mainly in theatrical terms, with reading as a subsidiary. But various difficulties arise immediately: many people can seldom if ever *see* first-rate plays, and are therefore precluded from enjoying drama if it is to be experienced only on the stage; some dramas are virtually 'unactable' like *Samson Agonistes*; and many plays, including some of the greatest, yield their full meaning only with the closest study. Moreover, each period tends to reinterpret the great plays of the past, in ways which suit its general preoccupations. Thus Shakespeare was largely rewritten in the eighteenth century to suit the taste of contemporary audiences; there was a notorious version of *King Lear* with a happy ending, and it is hard to imagine *Macbeth* played in eighteenth-century wigs and ruffles. In the same way the early nineteenth century, though it restored the original Shakespeare text, made more and more elaborate productions with greater and greater emphasis on visual lavishness. Later, and counter to this, there was a trend towards playing Shakespeare in conditions as closely imitative of the Elizabethan theatre as possible, and this has sometimes seemed falsely antiquarian and artificial. While there is obviously something good in the lively way in which each period takes from such a playwright what it can make use of, there is no doubt that the plays themselves were gravely distorted in the process.

This last statement may suggest a way of looking at the relation between the printed play and the acted one. Any production which leads us away from 'the words on the page' is *ipso facto* a bad one, whatever other merits it may have: the play *is* what the playwright wrote, and in the case of Shakespeare (for example) all we have left of his work; and though each new production should and in a sense must reinterpret the play, an acid test that can always be applied is that the visual and oral elements in the play lead towards the text. We cannot say flatly that *Macbeth* in modern dress (with field officers in steel helmets, and machine guns at Dunsinane) is absurd—it may even be that a new dimension can be added to our understanding of the play by such devices; we cannot even say that to perform *King Lear* in costume and *décor* reminiscent of the Japanese theatre is in itself wrong, but we can reasonably suspect such devices. This criterion can be seen at its simplest when a finely mounted play is not fully audible: the performance is then a bad one, whatever its other merits.

This leads us on to suggest how the most can be got out of a drama by schools. Probably the ideal sequence—seldom attainable in practice—is to read the play quickly, alone or in class, possibly even before it can be fully understood; then to study it in detail, trying to see the full implications; then to see a good production; and then to relate the production to one's knowledge of the play and examine critically where the acted play really enlightened, where it gave new insight, where it blurred what one had found in the text, and so use the production as a test of one's reading and the printed play as a test of what was offered on the stage. A sort of cross-fertilization then occurs, if the production was good; and even if it was bad, the effort involved in discovering where and how increases one's total grasp of the play. Certainly any opportunities offered of seeing a play one is studying should be taken, and radio and television versions, though they sometimes contain aberrations, are often valuable. Perhaps best of all is to take part in a production of a play one is also studying. The process of trying to find how to say a great speech and what movement and gesture correspond to it is enlightening. To act in such a play and to help in its production is fascinating, and often forces one into the heart of its meaning.

The history of drama is a very complex matter which we cannot attempt to go into here. The origins of English drama may well be in developments of certain elements of the church Mass; certainly all the earliest plays of which we know are religious—and some of them, notably the cycles of mystery plays produced by certain craft guilds, are very fine and well worth studying now. But the history of English drama is discontinuous, and it is not possible to trace an unbroken development as one can, say, in poetry since Elizabethan times, and in the novel since the mid-eighteenth century. There is one great period of flowering, from about

1580 to 1640; an apparently lively but not very rewarding period during the Restoration; the solitary and mildly interesting figure of Sheridan in the eighteenth century; and then nothing that is likely to engage our attention until a notable revival of serious drama in the present century, which dates from the middle fifties, and is still continuing full of energy and drive. Within the limits of this book, which is concerned with imaginative writing, the word 'drama' will mean Elizabethan and Jacobean drama, with occasional references to modern plays; and the fact that nine-tenths of our choices of dramatic passages come from Shakespeare is no more than the reflection of his absolute eminence, and the almost solitary eminence of the period in which he wrote. There is much else of interest, especially among Shakespeare's contemporaries, many of whom would be far better known but for his dominating and overshadowing figure; but there is nothing as worth detailed examination, and after 1660 the field is thin indeed. One can almost say that Shakespeare *is* English drama, at any rate so far.

Just as the world of fiction is bedevilled by strictly venal and commercial writers and publishers, so the world of drama is bedevilled by the concept of 'the box office.' With this we are not directly concerned except to note that counting heads, or seats, is no way of determining merit: if it were, the function of criticism would indeed vanish and statisticians could take over the work. There is a great deal of lively experiment going on in the modern theatre, but there is no doubt that most plays actually shown at any one time, in London or the provinces, are, as imaginative works, worthless. This applies equally to amateur drama, which is in itself a valuable social activity and in some areas a genuinely creative one; the fact is that most one-act plays are threadbare and impoverished in idea and in style, and when a full-length play is attempted, the company often feels an obligation to 'cover their costs' by producing a box-office success which will at least guarantee them adequate audiences. Thus the vicious circle continues; but at least there is no need for schools or students to become victims of it, since we are not obliged to 'count heads,' however much the commercial theatre has to do so.

'Drama,' then, as the word is used here, is quite distinct from 'theatre.' 'Drama' consists of imaginative works written for the stage but worthy of, and necessitating, close study in print. Few current successes will stand up to such scrutiny, and to call them 'good theatre' is often to define their limitations from our point of view, because the phrase tends to mean that they are immediately effective to a mass audience—that they produce a strong simple reaction in terms of a 'show.' Certainly a really good production will be 'good theatre' in the sense that its major effects will link the visual and the auditory—the gesture, movement, pose, grouping of the actors concerned with the imaginative concept of the dramatist himself; but the primary need is that it shall be 'good drama,' and this forces us back to the play as literature.

One further way of showing the primacy of the words becomes obvious when we reflect that Elizabethan plays were performed on bare boards by daylight. The Egyptian court in *Antony and Cleopatra*, the storm in *King Lear*, the sleep-walking scene with the candle in *Macbeth* were presented with little or no visual help, and one can say that it was this that gave the language its power. Modern dramatists often write lengthy italicized passages to give instructions to the actors, and exploit the elaborate facilities of staging and lighting which the modern theatre affords; but Shakespeare and his contemporaries evoke scene and atmosphere and spectacle almost solely through the spoken word. The spectacle, therefore, is valid only when it casts light on and brings out these words; and it is never indispensable, at any rate with a great play, because the words themselves do the work of the producer for our imaginations.

Even if we limit our attention to plays as literature, there are still many difficulties. If we use the plays of Shakespeare as examples, all we actually have is a series of speeches. The act and scene divisions and much of the instructions to actors printed, generally in italics, are additions by editors later than Shakespeare: only the barest exits and entrances are in the original texts. From this an enormous body of criticism and commentary has been developed, and a history of Shakespeare studies will show aberrations parallel to those of the performances mentioned above. This is not the place even to summarize this history, but one point of importance should be made. A writer called Morgann wrote a book on the character of Falstaff, and this was the first of a series of critical works which concentrated increasingly on the characters of Shakespeare's plays, more and more ignoring thematic and poetic elements in the pursuit of character analysis. These critics, treating the plays mainly as *psychological* masterpieces, tended to treat the personalities of the plays as if they existed apart from the speeches they made. This produced some absurdities, one of the most notorious of which is Mrs Jameson's *Girlhood of Shakespeare's Heroines*, in which Rosalind and Viola and Beatrice are provided with childhoods, which are then discussed and analysed in remorseless detail. This kind of criticism culminates in the often brilliant but often misleading *Shakespearean Tragedy* of A. C. Bradley. It is only in the last twenty-five years or so that Shakespearean criticism has been freed from this exclusive preoccupation with character, and a good deal of work has been done in considering other aspects—the themes of the plays and their relation to the thought of Shakespeare's time, and above all a detailed consideration of the poetry, not solely for the light it casts on character, but for the patterns it makes, the imagery it embodies, the total experience it evokes. This is not to suggest that the study of character is irrelevant: on the contrary, some plays, like *Othello*, have issues of character at their very root: but others, like *The Winter's Tale*, cannot be said to 'make sense' if the ordinary kind of character-analysis is the sole weapon, though they offer quite other values which make them great plays. The conclusion that modern criticism leads towards is, again, that the final basis of any judgment is in, and only in, the words on the page. Plays like Shakespeare's greatest are such powerful and evocative works that it is fatally easy to go off into emotional or philosophical disquisitions about them: and this process can only be kept in control by being sure always that any statement one makes can be endorsed from the text itself.

Shakespeare is pre-eminently the greatest dramatist, and the greatest poet, of our literature or of any other, and the way in which we approach his works is therefore of the greatest importance. The three hundred and fifty years that divide us from him (though they naturally cause some difficulties, particularly in language), seem insignificant; his understanding, sympathy, and penetration are great enough for his plays to speak to us, in our totally different environment, as clearly as they did to his contemporaries.

Only the briefest reference can be made here to recent developments in English drama—which represent perhaps the healthiest growing-point of the last ten years. Among the most interesting and original of recent playwrights are the following, and after each name I have suggested a play which will be found worth *reading* as well as seeing: Osborne (*Look Back in Anger*), Wesker (*Roots*), Pinter (*The Caretaker*), Arden (*Serjeant Musgrave's Dance*), Saunders (*Next Time I'll Sing to You*), Simpson (*A Resounding Tinkle*).

GENERAL CONCLUSIONS

The three great forms of imaginative literature, then, are poetry, drama, and fiction. All of these are indispensable and are bound to be at the centre of any course of imaginative reading. But there is a great deal of other important material which verges on the imaginative: the essay, non-fictional satire, expository prose of various kinds, philosophical prose, criticism, letters, diaries. A few examples from this vast field are given later, and it is only because of shortage of space that it is not discussed here: it is outside the scope of the present book. Nevertheless, it should be said that just as a diet of fiction alone, even good fiction, tends to spoil the palate, so the reading of imaginative literature should be interspersed with the reading of other kinds of prose, not only for the light it casts on imaginative literature itself, or for its own inherent interest, but also as a relief to the demands that the greatest works of imagination make on us.

Implicit throughout this chapter has been the contrast between the commercial success and the work of real merit. To mention only recent work, the contrast is seen in fiction between the average 'best-seller' and the novels of Lawrence or Forster; in poetry between the 'lyric' of the latest popular song and the best poems of Yeats; in drama between the latest bedroom farce and, say, *Murder in the Cathedral.* The works we are concerned with cannot any longer be said to be 'popular.' There is a deep and increasing cleavage between Art, which is the concern of a relatively tiny minority, and Entertainment, mass-produced for mass audiences. It is only too easy to imagine that the gulf was always as wide as it is now, that the division between 'highbrow' tastes and 'popular' tastes is natural and inevitable; but it is important to realize that this is not so. It is approximately true to say that the most popular novels from 1740 to 1840 were also the good novels: the publication of Mrs Henry Wood's *East Lynne* in 1861 may be regarded as the first occasion when a really popular work of fiction was almost totally without merit, and Dickens was the last great novelist who was also popular in the sense of being devotedly read by nearly every one who *could* read. When Johnson said of Gray's *Elegy written in a Country Church-yard* that he "rejoiced to concur with the opinion of the majority" about the poem's merits, he really meant the majority of those who could read at all. Even to-day there are occasional instances—perhaps, for example, in the films of Chaplin—where informed criticism and mass approval coincide, and the territories of art and entertainment overlap and merge for a moment. It may be that only large social changes and much improved education can ever again bring about a fusing of these two apparent opposites; but even if concern with art has to be a minority movement at present, it is worth insisting that for those really interested in art, what is currently known as entertainment doesn't in the main entertain, and the art, because it entertains *them*, becomes entertainment.

If I have not previously raised the vexed question of content versus style it is because the separation inferred seemed to me unhelpful and sometimes dangerous. If style and form are isolated from content, some very odd results occur, and we get absurdities like *The Decline of the Sonnet* or *The Heyday of the Octosyllabic Couplet* offered as chapter headings in histories of literature. It is the practice throughout this book to try to discover meaning, in its fullest sense, in any piece of writing, and discoveries about style can follow this close reading, which is always *for* content: one wishes to discover what the writer is saying, and one discovers both *what* and *how* simultaneously. If style is "a thinking out into language," then a thorough enough examination of the meaning will reveal the style in a single apprehension.

This chapter may reasonably conclude with two very general observations. First, though there is throughout this chapter and throughout this book an insistence on the need to scrutinize our material, and on the idea that only the closest examination yields the full meaning of great poems or plays or novels, this is not to suggest that there is really only one mode of reading, and that all others are unworthy. Reading should be extensive as well as intensive, discursive as well as concentrated, quick as well as slow, general as well as particular; there should be bulk as well as quality. Much of what we need to and should read would neither demand nor stand up to such close analysis, and a great deal of relatively quick, relatively unanalytical reading will and should be done, side by side with the much closer study that the greatest works need.

Finally, the point of reading great literature is really that life is very short, and that there is a strict limit, even in most fortunate circumstances, to the direct contacts we may make with first-class minds and first-class sensitivities. We may be lucky enough to number some of such minds among our personal friends; but a shelf of books enables us to know the most splendid minds of the past and the present with real intimacy. The pleasure and the understanding that this can give us is the personal gift that reading brings, and through reading the quality of our own lives can be improved, its satisfactions deepened, its inevitable limitations faced, its rewards intensified. All great literature, whatever its individual message, has this effect—that it *braces* us: it is always 'on the side of life.' We are, moreover, not only solitary beings but social animals. It is a commonplace that the contemporary crisis consists of a unique advance in techniques coupled with a primitive incapacity to solve the problems of living together in one world. Nearly all the technical problems we face are solved or in process of being solved, and yet we do not know how to live. Every day our newspapers present, side by side, some great advance in technology and some retreat into savagery, war, or racial hysteria. Man can control everything except himself. Anything, therefore, which contributes to a real understanding of others is precious. We shall be less easily stampeded by specious propaganda, less easily stirred to crude emotions, less easily prone to cruelty or thoughtlessness, if we are educated in this deepest sense of the word, educated in our hearts and minds to understanding others. It is in the belief that imaginative reading plays an essential part in such a process that this book has been written.

Topics for discussion or further activity

1. Discuss the use you make of public or other libraries. When you visit the library, do you go to 'find a book,' or with a definite book or subject in mind? Do you use a library for research? Have you generally found what you wanted? What improvements would you like to see in the public or school libraries you use?

2. Have you a library of your own? What are its chief contents? Do you buy books? Fiction or others? New or second-hand? Is there a second-hand bookshop in your town? If there is, do you use it often? Do you keep a "wants list"? Imagine you are given five pounds to spend on books: list the books you would buy.

3. What kind of fiction do you at present enjoy? Write a brief criticism of the novel you have most enjoyed. Do you read 'thrillers' or detective stories? What exactly do you get out of them? What works of fiction are you planning to read next year?

4. Make a case, in the form of a short speech, for or against any novelist of established reputation. Make some close references to the novels, including quotation. Which of the novels you have read as school-texts have you enjoyed? Which have you disliked? Why, exactly? (An informal debate could be arranged where the members of a class have read the same novel fairly recently.)

5. What poetry have you read on your own? What books of poetry do you posses? Have you recently heard poetry read on the radio? If so, what opinions did you form?

6. Read aloud to the class a poem you like and follow this with a short commentary. Produce a personal anthology of the twelve poems you like best. Prepare a talk on any poet whose work you like, and read some of his work aloud.

7. A group of students could jointly prepare a small collection of poems that have something in common: a particular period (Elizabethan, 'metaphysical,' 'romantic,' Victorian)—a particular writer or a particular kind of poem (satire, humorous verse, the ballad, the love lyric, 'nature' poetry) or particular subject-matter (war poetry, religious poetry, animals, flowers, industry, childhood, parodies). These should be introduced by one of the group to the class, and then read aloud by its members.

8. Write a review of any professional or amateur dramatic production you have seen, or make a speech describing it to the class. If the whole class can attend a performance of such a production, members can be asked beforehand to prepare to speak briefly to the class on some aspect of the production: the leading actors and their interpretations, stage design and sets, music if any, lighting, speech, movement, crowd scenes, interpretation of the dramatist's intention, etc.

9. Have you ever acted in a school or other amateur production? If so, what did you gain from the experience? Describe your problems and difficulties and how you overcame them. What play would you like to take part in, and which part would you like? Are you interested in the production side—costume, stage management, lighting, make-up? Why?

10. Discuss the relative merits of a play you have read and its performance, a novel dramatized or turned into a film or television play, a play you have seen in two different productions.

11. Outline how you would produce a play you have studied in class. Give a short talk to the class on what major problems in production you see; draw sketches of the sets you would like. If this is found to be too ambitious, discuss in some detail how you would produce one scene from a play studied in class—acting, gestures, and grouping, voice production, music or sound effects lighting, staging.

12. Write an essay, or give a talk, called "My Kind of Reading." Be absolutely frank and honest about your tastes, but try to support them by reasons and by detailed reference to the works you have enjoyed. An alternative plan is an essay or talk on "Reading I have disliked," again giving as much detail as you can, with quotation if possible.

Chapter Three

THE READING PROCESS IN SLOW MOTION

In this chapter an attempt is made to show the process of reading and appreciating at close quarters—in slow motion, as it were. I have found this a very difficult thing to do, because a good deal of the process is intuitive, and any attempt to 'show how it is done' may suggest imposing a technique, almost a drill, which would be quite foreign to the flexible and receptive state of mind that is needed. So it is essential at this point to offer the proper warnings—that no one should or indeed can impose a method of reading as such, and that anything here that gives the appearance of schematizing the reading process is dangerous. The following material is offered, therefore, tentatively, as a means of bridging the difficult early stages when there may be doubt as to how to set about examining a piece of writing, and certainly not to impose a method which will always apply.

The first poem chosen is *Adlestrop*, by Edward Thomas.

Yes. I remember Adlestrop—
The name, because one afternoon
Of heat the express-train drew up there
Unwontedly. It was late June.

The steam hissed. Someone cleared his throat.
No one left and no one came
On the bare platform. What I saw
Was Adlestrop—only the name

And willows, willow-herb, and grass,
And meadowsweet, and haycocks dry,
No whit less still and lonely fair
Than the high cloudlets in the sky.

And for that minute a blackbird sang
Close by, and round him, mistier,
Farther and farther, all the birds
Of Oxfordshire and Gloucestershire.

It is often a good idea to read the poem through quickly the first time, and a skilled reader will pick up some general pointers at this stage. It must then certainly be read aloud, at least once. Nearly all creative writing demands this, and poetry above all, since so much of its total impact depends on the relationship of sound and sense. A trial reading aloud, or perhaps several readings, will make clear and recognizable structural elements in the poem which do not immediately come through the eye. Thus in *Adlestrop* what we see on the page is four similar verses, rhyming in the second and fourth lines—four verses, one might say, of equal weight and similar structure. As soon as one reads it aloud one discovers that there is an important difference—that the first two verses are hesitant, broken (if you like, conversational in tone), and that the last two, in contrast, flow smoothly and continuously. You can learn to make this sort of discovery with the inner ear by a sort of internal 'mouthing,' which will quickly show what sort of reading the poem requires. Punctuation, and grammatical syntax, impose a particular sort of reading.

Here, then, we have two hesitant verses and two assured verses—or, to put it another way, two fragmented conversational verses and two flowing lyrical verses; and if we can discover why, we shall be near the central feeling of the poem.

Now, if we look at the first two verses more closely, we see that the whole process of thought begins with the *name*: in lines one and two: "I remember Adlestrop—The name" and again in line eight: "Adlestrop—only the name." If we ask ourselves why there is this emphasis on the name the poet offers the answer: he has seen the name of the village on a railway sign, and all he can remember is the actual look of the name in the village station—at least, at first. Once we have established the hesitant rhythms of the opening verses we are in a position to look more closely at them. An early question that will arise is why the poem starts with the single word "Yes." It obviously answers a question in conversation: the poet hears the name of the village and is perhaps asked whether he knows it. The name is familiar somehow to him, but at present evades a full memory: he sees it as it were out of the corner of his eye, and strives to grasp the memory. On a hot afternoon he is travelling in an express train towards the south-west and it draws up, perhaps because of signals, at a remote village station which would generally be served only by local trains. "Unwontedly" means of course 'unaccustomedly.' He can so far remember the heat, and the season, late June.

Verse two starts with two statements about sound. Anyone who has travelled long distances by rail knows the mysterious silence that descends when a familiar and habitual sound stops: in the same way a clock stops ticking, and you are subtly aware that you have been hearing it before though unaware of it. The noise of the express stops and you are immediately aware of the hissing steam, and in the sudden strange quiet your ears are attuned to even such a trifling sound as some one, perhaps in the next carriage, clearing his throat. There is no bustle of coming and going to confuse this peace and aural awareness, because the train wasn't intended to stop there at all. The poet looks out of the window, in memory, and sees the great staring name of the station: "*only* the name" and "the *bare* platform" both suggest emptiness. Then, as the memory floods back, he remembers looking beyond or behind the sign to the pastoral landscape: first a sort of close-up of the plants; willows and willow-herb (codlins-and-cream) suggest water-meadows or rivers in the valley behind, as does meadowsweet; and then the eye travels up to the slope beyond to see the contrasting haycocks *dry*—the heaps or piles of hay on the further slope, each separate and motionless in the heat, dotting the hillside in a way that 'echoes' the similarly ragged-edged, separate cloudlets in the sky which backs the hillside.

But the sounds have not been forgotten. In the minute that the train stops by the platform he hears a single blackbird somewhere quite near, and then, his hearing sharpened by the sudden silence after the rumbling noises of the train, he is aware of a rich patterning of sound stretching out into the distance behind the clear song of the blackbird—a territory of bird song, as it were, "mistier," more distant, the whole countryside bursting with song. The last line with its delightful 'misty' rhyme "Gloucestershire—mistier," places the village topographically as on the border of the two counties. The poet doesn't 'know' Adlestrop, as perhaps the questioner does, but he has caught its essence in these last verses: a landscape like many another, and yet tied in his memory to the one specific and evocative name which stared at him throughout this little fragment of experience, and which the name re-creates in memory.

We are now in a position to see that the apparent similarity of the four verses embodies and frames a movement from hesitation to assurance, from speech to feeling, from the physical description of a minor experience to an imaginative grasp. The poem moves with a remarkable fidelity and delicacy; its movement is found to be true of a range of such small but significant experiences, and to re-create the process by which a memory is recaptured. The tantalizing half-memory of the opening stanzas, we now find, moves into the fullness of the last two, from an empty memory ("the bare platform," "only the name") to the visual richness and particularity of verse three, and to the aural pattern of verse four. Adlestrop becomes for the poet, and through him for us, a symbol of a particular kind of pastoral landscape—quiet, "lonely fair" like the haycocks and the clouds, and bird-haunted. It is, in its minor way, a fine achievement.

The other poem chosen for 'slow-motion' analysis is *The Garden*, by Andrew Marvell.

How vainly men themselves amaze
To win the palm, the oak, or bays;
And their incessant labours see
Crowned from some single herb or tree,
Whose short and narrow-vergèd shade
Does prudently their toils upbraid;
While all flow'rs and all trees do close
To weave the garlands of repose.

Fair Quiet, have I found thee here,
And Innocence, thy sister dear!
Mistaken long, I sought you then
In busy companies of men.
Your sacred plants, if here below,
Only among the plants will grow.
Society is all but rude,
To this delicious solitude.

No white nor red was ever seen
So amorous as this lovely green.
Fond lovers, cruel as their flame,
Cut in these trees their mistress' name

Little, alas, they know or heed
How far these beauties hers exceed!
Fair trees! wheres'e'er your barks I wound,
No name shall but your own be found.

When we have run our passions' heat,
Love hither makes his best retreat.
The gods, that mortal beauty chase,
Still in a tree did end their race.
Apollo hunted Daphne so,
Only that she might laurel grow;
And Pan did after Syrinx speed,
Not as a nymph, but for a reed.

What wond'rous life is this I lead!
Ripe apples drop about my head;
The luscious clusters of the vine
Upon my mouth do crush their wine;
The nectarine and curious peach
Into my hands themselves do reach;
Stumbling on melons as I pass,
Ensnared with flow'rs, I fall on grass.

Meanwhile the mind, from pleasure less,
Withdraws into its happiness;
The mind, that ocean where each kind
Does straight its own resemblance find;
Yet it creates, transcending these,
Far other worlds and other seas;
Annihilating all that's made
To a green thought in a green shade.

Here at the fountain's sliding foot
Or at some fruit-tree's mossy root,
Casting the body's vest aside,
My soul into the boughs does glide;

There like a bird it sits and sings,
Then whets and combs its silver wings;
And, till prepared for longer flight,
Waves in its plumes the various light.

Such was that happy garden-state,
While Man there walked without a mate.
After a place so pure and sweet,
What other help could yet be meet!
But 'twas beyond a mortal's share
To wander solitary there;
Two paradises 'twere in one
To live in Paradise alone.

How well the skilful gardener drew
Of flow'rs and herbs this dial new;
Where from above the milder sun
Does through a fragrant zodiac run;
And as it works th'industrious bee
Computes its time as well as we.
How could such sweet and wholesome hours
Be reckoned but with herbs and flowers!

The poem should be read through, fairly quickly, then aloud, a good deal more slowly, to see how far the sound will help, and then more slowly to oneself. Even the first quick reading will reveal that we have here a far more complex piece than Edward Thomas's poem (though that, too, turned out to have a good deal more in it than might at first have been suspected). This poem is a great deal longer—and therefore has more room, as it were, for development; it deals with a whole elaborate response rather than a single and relatively simple experience; its language is that of the seventeenth century, and there are specific difficulties to be met here and there; it has classical references which we may need to look up; and it may be totally incomprehensible in places even when these purely referential or verbal difficulties have been overcome. Verse six may be found so, even though the movement and language may well be found beautiful at a first reading.

It is far harder to know where to start with a poem on this scale than with a short lyric like *Adlestrop*, if only because the latter is short enough to be able to be held in the mind as a unit after a few readings. Much more skill is needed to be able to do that with a poem of this length and complexity; indeed, even those who know the poem by heart and have constantly read it for years will continue to find deeper and richer 'layers' of meaning in it, and can often retain in the mind only a general flavour. So it is probably best not to try at this stage to make generalizations about such a poem beyond the very broad ones offered above, which will come naturally from the early readings. But we shall also by now have noted that, though the range of the poem seems vast, its rhythmic pattern and its rhymes seem simple and restricted: it may be surprising to note that as far as length of line is concerned it is identical with *Adlestrop*: both are written in octosyllabics or lines of eight syllables. But the total effect is so different—even though both are concerned broadly with the solaces of 'nature'—that we may reasonably conclude that to use the stick-on label 'octosyllabic couplet' will not help us very much. The question of the verse form, which we cannot help having noted early, is one to which we shall return later. We must now look at the poem in detail, patiently, extracting its meaning.

The first verse consists of one extended sentence and begins with an exclamation:

How vainly men themselves amaze
To win the palm, the oak, or bays.

We are pulled up by the word "amaze," which is clearly not used entirely in a modern sense. Here it means something like 'confuse,' 'perplex,' 'agitate,' rather than 'astonish': the word 'maze' helps to show the meaning. "To win the palm" is clear enough, and leads us on to see that "the oak" and "the bays" are other symbols of worldly success or honour: the palm a symbol of glory, particularly military glory, the oak perhaps of royalty, the bays of poetry or the arts. Men, then, work incessantly throughout their life to achieve a crown or garland of one tree, which when put on their head offers only a "short and narrow-vergèd shade," only the slightest shade, which wisely points out the absurdity of their labours ("Does prudently their toils upbraid"): meanwhile "All flow'rs and all trees" close over your head and offer you the crown or garland of rest and quietness, away from the blazing forum or market-place where worldly success has been gained. The desperate pursuit of most men, says Marvell, is towards an objective the highest reward of which is a few branches from a *single* herb or tree; if they had been more sensible they would have forgone public triumph, retired to the garden in a spirit of peacefulness, and found themselves crowned by *all* the plants and trees there are. The wit of this first verse—Marvell, though entirely serious, is also amused at the 'trick' by which he has made the case—is a pointer to what is to follow.

Verse two starts with two personifications; "Quiet" and "Innocence" are seen as people. For many years ("then") he has pursued these objectives of life which he claims are the final ones, in the hurly-burly of society ("In busy companies of men"). The plants which are sacred to quiet and innocence will grow only in natural surroundings, among other plants, and should never have been expected in any other setting. "If here below" may worry us for a moment, until we see that it is a sort of shorthand for 'if, indeed, they can be found on this earth at all, and not only in heaven.' Human society—he is thinking perhaps of the court and polite society particularly—is inelegant, rough, indeed almost barbarous ("all but rude") compared with the delicious solitude that the garden offers. A very strong antithesis here has lost some of its force now: but in Marvell's time 'society' would tend to despise rural life as crude and rough; and here, as so often throughout this poem, Marvell stands the idea, with consummate neatness, on its head.

The next verse shows an increase in this controlled wit. One of the pleasures that solitude will cut one off from is love, and the verse starts with the bold assertion that the green of the garden is more "amorous" than any white or red—the colours of human flesh. Lovers ("fond" means 'foolish') cut on the bark of the trees the name of the woman they love—a practice that is still often seen, with initials and lovers' hearts—and in the process show as much cruelty as the cruel flame of passion which is consuming them. They fail to notice, so absorbed are they, that the tree they are wounding is far more beautiful than the beauty they claim to be celebrating. The verse ends with a delicious twist when the poet declares that if the bark must be cut into, the only justification would be to carve the name of the tree on it, since that alone names a beauty commensurate with the harm that might be done. The "I" in the last line but one carries a stress, and distinguishes him from the cruel lover: he is unlikely ever to wound a tree, but if he did so the result would be like the labels one may see on trees in large parks.

The next verse again functions as a unit. Love, having exhausted itself in human passion, comes to the garden as to a "retreat"; in this last word there are religious overtones, and "heat," as well as meaning 'intensity,' carries also the meaning of a section of a race: thus the garden becomes the final objective of the race of love. The metaphor from running is sustained with the generalization about the ancient gods, who pursued mortal maidens but always ("still") ended with a tree. With sublime impudence he proceeds to 'prove' this by two references to classical mythology, which may need a word of explanation. Apollo, the god of the sun and of poetry, fell in love with the nymph Daphne, and pursued her until at the last moment she was transformed through the intervention of a goddess into a laurel bush, which he found himself grasping when he thought he had caught her; *Daphne* is still the Latin name for certain species of laurel. Similarly Pan, god of nature and shepherds, pursued the chaste water-nymph Syrinx who, again at the last moment, became metamorphosed into a reed. Pan, in despair, cut down the reeds and made of them pan-pipes on which he played melodies to express his love. But Marvell pretends that Apollo's only object was to have Daphne transformed into a laurel and that Pan's consummation came when Syrinx became a reed; these inversions of the story are of course in line with the general claim that 'nature' is in every way superior to humanity: even the gods think so.

Verse five, continuing with the theme of love versus nature, moves away from the witty play with mythology to a personal immediacy of experience. The rich fruitfulness of the garden is stressed, and it will take several readings before we see that this is more than a mere catalogue of fruits, but is also a series of metaphors of love itself, showing that the garden offers all that human love offers. Lines three and four, for example, are metaphors for kissing as well as apt descriptions of the taste and sensation of the grapes. The nectarine and peach ("curious" here means 'rare') remind one of the human skin ('a skin like a peach' is a common enough expression) and the fruits offer themselves ("Into my hands themselves do reach"). The verse ends with the ecstasy of physical love transformed into terms of plants and fruit.

A full treatment of the very difficult verse six is not possible or appropriate here,[1] but the general sense may be suggested. The body is in an ecstasy of happiness and fulfilment (verse five); "meanwhile" the mind, not satisfied merely with *pleasure* (which suggests something temporary), withdraws—from society, even from its surroundings—into the much solider and more permanent state of *happiness.* The mind is like an unlimited ocean where the power of analogy and comparison in respect of the real world and one's real surroundings, is limitless, but which is capable of going beyond ("transcending") these processes and creating worlds and oceans of its own, reducing the whole of the world of phenomena ("all that's made") "to a green thought in a green shade." The delicious coolness of this suggests in richer terms than ever before in the poem, how the garden is the end and objective of everything else. One's thoughts are "green," living, unstrained, 'natural,' in such surroundings, and acquire the leafy, budding naturalness and branching proliferations of the plants themselves.

The next verse moves from the ground ("I fall on grass") imaginatively into the trees themselves. In this mood of unity with nature and of complete physical well-being and relaxation, the soul can cast aside the body which is its garment ("the body's vest"), and as the poet looks up into the trees from below, he imagines his soul being as close to them as a bird, as easy and natural as the bird singing, sitting on the nest, and arranging its feathers; and before it finally leaves the body in death ("till prepared for longer

[1] For a much fuller analysis, see William Empson's essay in *Some Versions of Pastoral.*

flight") the changing flickering ("various") light of the myriad leaves is cast on its feathers, and it is totally embodied into its surroundings: "Waves in its plumes the various light."

Another reflective verse follows. Not satisfied with introducing Greek mythology, Marvell now, with perfect dignity and tact, and yet with an extraordinary audacity, proceeds to take the story of the Garden of Eden and transform it for his own purposes. The state of solitude and bliss he has been describing only existed in perfection when Adam was there before the creation of Eve. "Garden-state" suggests a kingdom which is also a garden, and also a kind of splendour as in the expression 'the king is *in state*.' Paradise was so perfect that no other "help could yet be meet"—a reference to the description, in *Genesis*, of Eve as "an help meet for him (Adam)." But to be alone in such perfect surroundings was too good for any human being ("'twas beyond a mortal's share"), and though he remained in Paradise for a while with Eve it would have been a double Paradise to be allowed to remain there alone: so God provided Eve so that it should not be too perfect—and without actually saying so, the poet reminds us that the trouble started when Eve arrived and the Fall followed. But the major point is that the loneliness, to relieve which God provided Adam with a mate, is seen as a perfection for which man was not worthy: only God could have such unalloyed bliss.

The last verse can perhaps be viewed as something of an anticlimax after the splendour of the previous one. It refers to the seventeenth-century practice of making herb gardens planted in the form of a dial so that each bed represents one of the zodiacal signs, and the sun and the bees reckon time as they move across these beds. The passing hours are so blissful in the garden that clocks would be absurdly out of place: only herbs and flowers are appropriate means of registering the gentle passage of time.

This analysis has already become much too long, but it should now be possible to look back over this very complex and powerful poem and see how it is put together. Verses one and two condemn society and social ambition in contrast with the quietness and innocence of natural things. Verses three, four, and five show how the other great virtue of human contact, love, is made trifling and absurd by comparison with the rewards the garden offers, and incidentally claim that the garden's pleasures are like love, really *are* love, as well as quoting the ancient gods for support. Verse six shows that the vast power of the mind is satisfied, indeed enriched, by such a setting; verse seven that the garden frees not only the mind, but the soul. Verse eight summarizes and puts the particular claims of the rest of the poem into a truly vast historical and mythological perspective, and verse nine quietly concludes that time itself is gentler and sweeter among the plants.

The poem is a more extraordinary achievement when one sees that the poet is often witty or impudent, especially at the most serious moments, and enables one to conclude that seriousness and wit are not opposites, but may, in this sort of writing, be complementary facets of the same mind and the same sensibility; a great poet can be serious without being solemn. Finally the range of thought and feeling is all expressed in this apparently restricting short line, balanced, formalized and contained in the regular steady beat of the rhyming couplet. However inadequate the reading offered here, it may suggest that in some poetry, thought and feeling, intense emotion and audacious wit, beauty of language, rhythm and metre and a controlled amusement, are not in conflict but are unified in one expression.

Part Two

EXAMPLES OF CLOSE READING

THE next three chapters give detailed examinations of poems, passages from drama, and prose passages. The choice throughout was dictated by personal taste; thus, though there is little doubt that several of the poems examined, for example, are very great, they are not in any way offered as a collection of Great Poems, but as a personal selection of poems which have moved the writer. The same applies to the chapters on drama and prose. None of them attempts to cover *kinds* of poetry, drama or fiction, and they do not fall into any chronological or other pattern, though, naturally, it is hoped that they show a certain range.

The commentaries are not offered as 'models'—a dangerous conception where criticism is concerned, since if criticism is not in the end a *personal* judgment, it is nothing. Nor do they claim to be complete or exhaustive: not only do they fall short of what the original passages demand by way of commentary, but verse, drama, and prose of real quality is in the deepest sense inexhaustible. Where the inner organization of the original is elaborate, the commentary is correspondingly full: other and simpler passages have been given briefer analyses. In every case the aim is to show what a detailed reading can reveal.

The poems chosen are all complete except for the passage by Pope, which is an extract from a longer poem; the dramatic passages all come from Shakespeare; and five of the six prose passages are from novels.

Chapter Four

SOME POEMS EXAMINED

(I)

Tired with all these, for restful death I cry—
As, to behold Desert a beggar born,
And needy Nothing trimm'd in jollity,
And purest Faith unhappily forsworn,
And gilded Honour shamefully misplaced,
And maiden Virtue rudely strumpeted,
And right Perfection wrongfully disgraced,
And Strength by limping Sway disabled,
And Art made tongue-tied by Authority,
And Folly, doctor-like, controlling Skill,
And simple Truth miscalled Simplicity,
And captive Good attending captain Ill:
  Tired with all these, from these would I be gone,
  Save that, to die, I leave my love alone.

THIS is one of Shakespeare's magnificent sonnets. There are a hundred and fifty-four of them, many of which are worth the closest study, and this is No. 66 in the series. It is unusual in structure. The basic structure of the Shakespearean sonnet need not delay us for long. It is a poem of fourteen lines, which divides into three sets of four lines, rhyming *abab*, and a final rhymed couplet. Such is the poet's power that in this apparently narrow compass he can ring astonishing changes and strike some of the deepest notes in English poetry.

This poem begins with a sort of suspension—"Tired with all these"—and we are then offered a series of examples of "these," which go on accumulating till the final couplet, which gives the poet's only reason for living on. The middle of the poem consists of a series of personifications, each line showing the savage inequality of the times he lived in, and functioning by cumulative means as an indictment of the life of court and city, which he longs to leave but cannot. "As" in line two means roughly 'for example,' and the string of "ands" makes the picture blacker and blacker, until life in such circumstances seems unendurable. "Desert" means 'worthiness,' (as in 'he got his just deserts') and thus 'worthy people'; but they are born in beggary, while the "Nothing" ('No-thing'), perhaps the court favourite who is "needy" but worthless also, is fitted out ("trimmed") with superfluous decoration. Faith is ridiculed and tricked, Honour ("gilded" suggests that it is a mere show, just as in *King Lear* we read "Plate sin with gold, And the strong lance of justice hurtless breaks") is given only to the unworthy; "Virtue" is cruelly prostituted and so turned to vice; what is natural and just and right ("right Perfection") is brought into contempt: the implication is that what is *right* is made *wrong*. "Strength," the sturdy natural strength of honesty, is made impotent and powerless by "Sway," which is roughly what we now call 'influence,' and Sway is limping: in itself it is impotent, save that it has political power. "Art," the true voice of Art, is silenced ("tongue-tied") by those in authority, perhaps by censorship, and this prevents the artist from saying what he really means through fear of punishment, which could be severe indeed in Shakespeare's day. "Folly" (foolishness) controls Skill or ability, as a doctor controls a patient; the simple "Truth" (by a brilliant pun) is falsely labelled "Simplicity," that is naivety, as when we say nowadays 'he is a little simple.' Finally in this suffocating catalogue of inequity, cruelty, and vice in high places comes the summarizing line; all that is good is a slave ("captive Good") waiting in attendance on its master, all that is evil ("Captain Ill"). "Tired with all these" is then repeated, but with how different an emphasis: we now know in detail what "these" are, and the poem finishes with the declaration that his love alone prevents him from despair or death, both because it is the only note of sanity and beauty in a world that seems hideous and bestial, and because he cannot leave his love to face its temptations and cruelties without the poet's support.

As in so much great poetry, the structure is an inevitable (however original) means of embodying precisely this set of thoughts and feelings. The string of personifications, the remorseless series of "ands" leave us reeling as under a series of physical blows; no corner of life seems open to sweetness and justice; and the end gives with a simple poignancy the one factor that can keep the poet sane. Death indeed is restful in contrast with this appalling parade and is quietly evoked in "from these I would be gone": and suicide or oblivion is rejected on the sole ground of his love, which gives it great dignity and power, in that it can weigh more heavily in the balance than all the monstrosities of society.

This sonnet was chosen as offering in small compass a particular set of intensities: but it would be quite wrong to take it as typical of Shakespeare, either as a sonnet writer or in any other aspect. So wide is his range and so protean his mind that it seems almost universal; but other sonnets should be read as contrasts with this in mood, tone, and content.

(II)

The Owl

Downhill I came, hungry, and yet not starved;
Cold, yet had heat within me that was proof
Against the North Wind; tired, yet so that rest
Had seemed the sweetest thing under a roof.

Then at the inn I had food, fire, and rest,
Knowing how hungry, cold and tired was I.
All of the night was quite barred out except
An owl's cry, a most melancholy cry

Shaken out long and clear upon the hill,
No merry note, nor cause of merriment,
But one telling me plain what I escaped
And others could not, that night, as in I went.

And salted was my food, and my repose,
Salted and sobered, too, by the bird's voice
Speaking for all who lay under the stars,
Soldiers and poor, unable to rejoice.

The Owl was written by Edward Thomas, an English lyrical poet who was killed in the First World War. Its quiet thoughtful tone, its gentleness and sympathy, are distinctive and typical of this fine poet.

Edward Thomas evokes most beautifully the English landscape in prose and verse: but his landscapes are seldom or never landscapes for their own sake, and unlike that of many of his contemporaries—whose view of the countryside was over-lush and romanticized—his attitude is never merely descriptive, but always closely related to his own feelings and consciousness. He shows what has been called "a distinctively *modern* sensibility." He did a great deal of walking and this poem describes an interior experience of one of his walks.

He has been walking all day, one feels: he is hungry, cold and tired, but each of these sensations is modified. He is hungry but hunger is pleasant and not in any way desperate or extreme—"and yet not starved"; he is cold but has still enough body-heat, as it were, to withstand the onslaughts of the North Wind against which he had been walking; tired indeed, but not so tired that he cannot enjoy and take pleasure in the prospects of rest at the inn, the rest which in anticipation seems "the sweetest thing under a roof." At the inn where he is staying for the night he finds the food, fire, and rest he needs, and his pleasure in them is reinforced by the knowledge of this hunger, cold, and fatigue. Within the warm inn, the night with its memories of cold and hunger is "quite barred out," both literally in the sense that the inn door is barred, and metaphorically in the sense that the wind and cold outside seem remote in the cosy warmth around him. Only in one way can the 'outside' reach him —through sound. He hears the cry of an owl: he means the tawny owl whose note is often rendered 'tu-whit, tu-whoo,' with a long drawn out note at the end, generally with a quaver in it: this effect is magnificently rendered in "shaken out long and clear upon the hill." It is "a most melancholy cry" suggesting the cold autumnal or wintry weather outside ("the North Wind" also makes this point): and while it could increase his own sense of the surrounding comfort of the inn, he insists that it is "no merry note"—a reference to Shakespeare's song from *Love's Labours Lost*:

When blood is nipt, and ways be foul,
Then nightly sings the staring owl
Tu-whit! Tu-whoo! A merry note. . . .

But the note is not merry; it is a melancholy cry, and it causes no merriment in the poet, but tells him plainly what he escaped in the chill foreboding darkness outside on that particular night when he entered the comfort of the inn—"and others could not." Not for him the easy comfort: the owl's cry tells him that others have no such comforts as he is experiencing, but are still out in the wind and weather. "Salted"—a remarkable word—means that he simultaneously appreciated the food and repose more by virtue of what he had escaped from, and at the same time found it more valuable and satisfactory because others so needed it; yet his satisfaction is bitter in the reflection that these rich and simple pleasures were available to him only through privilege. His pleasure is "sobered," modified, the delight is mixed with a painful sympathy when the bird's voice reminds him by its poignancy of all who must sleep out under the stars on this bitter night: soldiers in tents or in trenches, and the tramps and gipsies 'sleeping rough,' who cannot, like the poet, rejoice in their escape—who have no roof, no warmth, perhaps no food, and no prospect of real rest. "Soldiers and poor" summarizes the under-privileged—and he knew, or was to know, what both groups had to endure.

The poem makes a statement of something that is simple and to which lip-service is often enough paid—the idea that one's thankfulness at the simple fulfilments of life, food, rest, and shelter after exhaustion and exposure, is and should be coloured by the recognition that it is a special privilege and that thousands in England and millions in the world cannot have it—a sympathy natural enough but seldom presented with such simplicity and power. The subtle hesitating rhythms (verse one, the relationship between lines eight and nine), the delicate precision of his awareness of his own bodily state in the first verse, and above all the use of the evocative power of the owl's cry, all make this a remarkable and beautiful poem, instinct with sympathy, honest in feeling and delicate in balance.

(III)

O Waly Waly

The water is wide, I cannot get o'er,
And neither have I wings to fly:
Give me a boat that will carry two,
And both shall row, my love and I.

O down in the meadows the other day
A-gathering flowers both fine and gay,
A-gathering flowers both red and blue,
I little thought what love can do.

I put my hand into one soft bush,
Thinking the sweetest flowers to find;
I pricked my finger right to the bone,
And left the sweetest flower behind.

I leaned my back against some oak
Thinking that he was a trusty tree;
But first he bended and then he broke,
And so did my false love to me.

A ship there is and she sails the sea,
She's loaded deep as deep can be,
But not so deep as the love I'm in,
I know not if I sink or swim.

O love is handsome and love is fine,
And love's a jewel when it is new,
But when it is old, it groweth cold,
And fades away like morning dew.

This is an anonymous English folk-song, part of the rich tradition the loss of which is one of the prices we pay for industrialization. It is included here to show with what power these early songs express themselves, and to imply by contrast the impoverishment of idea and feeling in most examples of the modern equivalent, the popular song.

Verses of this kind are very closely adjusted to the tune—in this case a very fine one; and a proper study of the verse involves an examination of its relationship to the melody. All that can be said here about this is that the melody rises to its highest point at the beginning of the third line, followed by a falling line moving more slowly, and each verse will be found to have its 'key' at that point (*e.g.*, "I pricked my finger," "But when it is old") and to fade away afterwards as in the last verse. The verbal pattern, the rise and fall of intensity, correspond with the emotional line of the music.

A detailed analysis of this delicate and charming lyric is not needed; but one or two points may be made. The poem could be sung by either a man or a woman, though the general feeling is of a deserted woman. It consists of a series of separate images each lasting for a verse, each derived from a pastoral background, and unified by the melodic and rhythmic pattern. There is a subtle interplay between the singer's recognition of her own deep feelings and her despair at the fate of such a love; thus verses 1, 2, and 5 with their warm positiveness are counterpoised against the dangers inherent in love (verse 3), the possible treachery of the loved one (verse 4), and the transitory nature of any love (verse 6). None of the images is 'explained' and there is a beautiful poised ambiguity about all of them. Thus in verse 1 the wide water can separate the lovers, and marriage be symbolized by the boat that will carry them over; verses 2 and 3 are linked together, the idyllic picture of the lovers picking flowers, the singer heavy with love, and the *double entendre* of the image about pricking the finger. The ship in verse 5 picks up the image in the opening lines and the last verse poignantly summarizes and generalizes the personal emotions of the rest.

Any community which can produce such poetry as part of a popular tradition—and this is only one of hundreds of equally fine folk songs—needs not fear comparison with a more literate and sophisticated culture. From this rich source all writers and composers before the nineteenth century drew some of their deepest and finest concepts; and to replace it we have at present little or no substitute.

(IV)

London

I wander thro' each charter'd street
   Near where the charter'd Thames does flow,
And mark in every face I meet
   Marks of weakness, marks of woe.

In every cry of every man,
   In every infant's cry of fear,
In every voice, in every ban,
   The mind-forg'd manacles I hear.

How the chimney-sweeper's cry
   Every black'ning church appals;
And the hapless soldier's sigh
   Runs in blood down palace walls.

But most thro' midnight streets I hear
  How the youthful harlot's curse
Blasts the new-born infant's tear
  And blights with plagues the marriage-hearse.

This poem belongs to the volume *Songs of Innocence and of Experience* by William Blake, a series of short poems contrasting the two states of mind: as he said, "Showing the Two Contrary States of the Human Soul." The *Songs of Experience*, from which this poem comes, are expressions of horror at the cruelties and savageries of civilization. It is odd that a poem so 'sociological' in content should demand so little by way of historical background. Indeed, the only background needed for the poem is to know that it was written probably in the 1780's or early 1790's and to have in one's mind a picture of what London, the first fully industrial city of the world, would be like at that time, when the Industrial Revolution was in its first great stride—what one writer calls the 'Eotechnic' period. But even this is not really necessary, because the poem offers its own description; and indeed, a walk through the industrial part of a modern city will yield a picture that is not entirely different.

The verse movement here is apparently simple and naive. Yet its restraint hides a powerful indictment. The word "charter'd," with its repetition, is of key importance. 'Chartered' means in the first place privileged or free, as if granted right by royal or other charter: in this meaning of the word the contrast between this privilege and splendour and the third and fourth lines is obvious. But 'chartered' can also evoke its opposite and come to mean 'restricted' or 'constrained'—the narrow confined streets of the city, the river itself pieced or farmed out, owned, as it is physically restricted by the warehouses, factories, and houses on its banks. When a ship is 'chartered' it is hired out for commercial purposes, and this meaning applies to the whole poem. The poet sees as he walks along these proud streets the faces 'signed' (as it were) by what is to him a hideous mode of life: they suggest every kind of frustration, sickness, and vice. In the second verse we move to the sounds of the city—the cry of sick or starving men, the cry of frightened children, the bans or prohibitions surrounding people on every side, the manacles, forged by society itself, in which man finds himself chained.

The chimney sweeper, often a child (as we can see from Blake's many other references) cries his trade and what he actually cries is "'weep! 'weep!" with its obvious ambiguity: his degraded and disease-borne life symbolizes the cruelty of man and "appals" or makes ridiculous and hypocritical the pretensions of the Church which tolerates such a social evil; "black'ning" refers to the soot-laden walls of the city churches. The soldier symbolizes war, the second great vice of society, parallel with the 'civilian' cruelty of the chimney-sweep, and the sigh he gives in his misery is a standing affront to the palace he is employed to defend and which brought him into being; so the splendid marble of the palace is stained with blood by his existence.

The third symbol is the young girl walking the midnight streets, and through her trade, which symbolizes the third cruelty of the city, lust, she brings despair and disease to the infant and to marriage itself. "The marriage-hearse" is a bitterly ironic use of opposites, and the usual associations of marriage clash with the funerary 'hearse' symbolizing not life but death.

The indictment is indeed a formidable one, though a reading of the history of the period will suggest that it is not exaggerated. Blake lived in London for much of his life, and his visionary eye pierces through the complacency and callousness of the time to the evil realities beneath its glitter and splendour. His own drawing accompanying this poem on its first publication shows a crippled beggar led by a child. The poem makes its impact precisely through the simplicity of tone and form, and a continual series of images which suggest 'staining' in some way: "marks," "blackening church," "runs in blood," "blasts," "blights." Throughout his life he retained a fresh vision, childlike in the best sense, of "what man has made of man," and his indictment of the early industrial city is a remarkable forecast of the whole social history of the last century and a half. It is also a useful corrective of romantic notions of the past.

(V)

During Wind and Rain

They sing their dearest songs—
He, she, all of them—yea,
Treble and tenor and bass
　And one to play;
With the candles mooning each face . . .
　Ah, no; the years O!
How the sick leaves reel down in throngs!

They clear the creeping moss—
Elders and juniors—aye,
Making the pathway neat
　And the garden gay;
And they build a shady seat . . .
　Ah, no; the years, the years;
See how the webbed white stormbirds wing across!

They are blithely breakfasting all—
Men and maidens—yea,
Under the summer tree
With a glimpse of the bay,
While pet birds come to the knee . .
Ah, no; the years O!
And the rotten rose is ript from the wall.

They move to a high new house,
He, she, all of them—aye,
Clocks and carpets and chairs
Out on the lawn all day,
And the brightest things that are theirs . . .
Ah, no; the years, the years;
Down their chiselled names the raindrop ploughs.

Thomas Hardy wrote this poem in 1913, at the age of seventy-three. He wrote poems as a young man, and then novels, largely for financial reasons; as an old man he went back to his first love, the writing of verse.

The poem looks back across a period of forty years to memories of his life as a young married man. He remembers their simple pleasures, the quiet winter evenings round the piano (verse 1), gardening (verse 2), meals out of doors (verse 3), and the excitement of moving house (verse 4). The first five lines of each verse offer these descriptions, in simple pure language, as simple and modest (and as fundamental) as the experiences themselves. The fifth and sixth lines of each verse make a recognition of the huge gap of time between then and now. The present tense is used throughout, but in two time-dimensions, as it were. The first is the 'historic present': the daily events of that early period are so vivid that they come to his mind in a present immediacy, only to be forced into the real present (the present tense of the writing of the poem). After the "Ah no," which recognizes, with a wrench, that the experiences are not now but then, a single line describes what he sees, I think, from his study window: and the last line of each verse is a picture of late autumn ("*During Wind and Rain*"), with the falling leaves, the gulls blown against the wind and flashing across the window, the old dead rose torn down from its supports, so lovingly made in the days of the past, and finally the raindrops collecting on the tombstones of those he loved and 'ploughing' with a sickening lurch down the names chiselled on the headstones.

The impact of this poem comes from the delicacy of its organization (the rhyme scheme is subtle and appropriate) and the complete lack of self-pity in the recognition of mortality and tragedy which the poet refuses to soften or sweeten; the early memories are sweet indeed ("dearest," "brightest") but they are held warmly in the mind and not sentimentalized. The last line of each verse contains the violent and indeed savage verbs, "reel," "wing," "ript," "ploughs," and the corresponding adjectives "sick," "storm," "rotten," "chiselled"; and there are many internal correspondences which enrich the experience the poem offers—the rotten rose "ript from the wall" in contrast with the careful lovingness of the work in the garden, the alien stormbirds in contrast with the tame pet birds that are fed with crumbs at the garden table, the summer tree full of light and shadow, contrasting with the sick leaves reeling in the autumn wind. The freshness of vision in the remembered patches of experience is remarkable: the grandfather clock on the lawn waiting to be moved to the "high new house," the candles on the piano sconces lighting the round surfaces of the faces of the singers at the piano ("mooning each face"). With the finely imagined and contrasting symbols of old age at the end of each verse, they contribute to a balanced and delicate lyric, which is very poignant without a hint of sentimentality or mere nostalgia.

(VI)

Pleasures the sex, as children birds, pursue,
Still out of reach, yet never out of view;
Sure, if they catch, to spoil the toy at most,
To covet flying, and regret when lost:
At last, to follies youth could scarce defend,
It grows their age's prudence to pretend;
Ashamed to own they gave delight before,
Reduced to feign it when they give no more:
As hags hold sabbats, less for joy than spite,
So these their merry, miserable night;
Still round and round the ghosts of beauty glide,
And haunt the places where their honour died.
See how the world its veterans rewards!
A youth of frolics, an old age of cards;
Fair to no purpose, artful to no end,
Young without lovers, old without a friend;
A fop their passion, but their prize a sot,
Alive, ridiculous, and dead, forgot!

This is part of an Epistle by Alexander Pope, dedicated to Mrs Martha Blount (No. 2 of *Moral Essays*). It contrasts strongly with most of the contents of this section, and is included mainly to illustrate how the imagination works in a poet whose terms of reference are intensely *social*. Pope is concerned primarily with the expression of a widely acceptable evaluation of social behaviour, and his weapon here is satire.

The poet is warning his 'correspondent' against the vapid emptiness of 'polite life,' the life of the wealthy and fashionable woman, her futile and repetitive pursuits and her pseudo-sophistication. The warning is made by a wickedly witty, and in places cruel description of her life. The rhymed couplets act as a formal enclosure within which this technically brilliant poet rings his changes of rhythm and emphasis.

The first four lines develop an elaborate comparison. "The sex" is a common phrase for 'the female sex.' They pursue pleasures as children pursue birds; the pleasure is never caught, yet constantly tantalizes by always being in sight. To catch the bird is to spoil the very object of the chase: the earthbound child, like the fashionable woman, envies the light movement of the bird, but spoils it by catching it (the bird is no longer really a bird, the pleasure evaporates in one's hand); or if it is allowed to escape, both feel a sense of loss (line four). The ageing woman of fashion claims to have committed follies that even young people (who might be more easily excused) would deplore; prudence, the traditional virtue of age, is counterpoised against the follies of youth. But the sting is in the tail: they are only, after all, 'pretending,' to give themselves a reputation of daring among the sophisticated. In the next couplet they sneer at their own youth ("ashamed to own") and its love-affairs ('how callow young people are!') but must now pretend to please their lovers, though in fact they fail. The witches' "sabbats" (their ceremonial dances held in secret at night) are compared with the balls and banquets of these women; what ought to be a joyful occasion is merely a spiteful one (the witches wish merely to spite their victims, not to enjoy themselves, and the women are gossiping and slandering spitefully); in "merry, miserable night," "merry" states their claim (that the dance was delightful) "miserable" the fact, and the juxtaposition of the two adjectives makes the night frenetically pleasure-seeking and fundamentally unfulfilling. They are going through the motions of pleasure, and in so far as "night" suggests the decline or evening of their own lives, it makes a comment on the frustration of their whole existence. A beautiful couplet follows ("Still round and round. . . ."), in which the ageing belles dance for ever, the mere ghosts of beauty, haunting (they can't keep away from such places) the ballrooms where they originally lost their honour in some empty love-affair, and are condemned to glide for ever in memory of its death.

The movement now changes to a more general, and even more devastating picture ("See how the world . . ."). The fate of the aged 'socialites' is seen with horrible clarity: their youth is spent in "follies," the futile round of pleasure, and their old age in playing cards in the ante-rooms while the younger ones dance. They have worked hard at improving their own beauty, but have never made any real use of it ("fair to no purpose"); they have used all their artifice (cosmetics, gowns, false mannerisms) in aid of no real object ("artful to no end"); when young they are too "artful" to win real love, in old age they lack the compensatory comfort of friendship. Even their highest ambition in youth was nothing but the love of one who was in fact a fop, but what they finish with is something even worse, a worn-out drunkard ("sot"). The last savage line 'places' them for ever: the absurdity of their life is balanced by the just oblivion that follows their death.

It is useful to remember that poetry concerns itself with all aspect of human experience; in schools it is often only the lyric, the expression of purely personal emotion, that is thought of as poetry. But this passage, and particularly its ending, is unmistakeably poetry of a high order. The balanced antitheses of the last five lines act as a series of hammer-blows enclosing the victim at each end of her life, and the furious contempt of the poet at the fatuities of society is all the more effective for being 'contained' in the dignified 'stepping' movement of the verse pattern. This makes even the scream at the end a controlled performance —a thing of formal beauty.

(VII)

The Starlight Night

Look at the stars! look, look up at the skies!
O look at all the fire-folk sitting in the air!
The bright boroughs, the circle-citadels there!
Down in dim woods the diamond delves! the elves'-eyes!
The grey lawns cold where gold, where quick-gold lies!
Wind-beat whitebeam! airy abeles set on a flare!
Flake-doves sent floating forth at a farmyard scare!—
Ah well! it is all a purchase, all is a prize.

Buy then! bid then!—What?—Prayer, patience, alms, vows.
Look, look: a May-mess, like on orchard boughs!
Look! March-bloom, like on mealed-with-yellow sallows!
These are indeed the barn; withindoors house
The shocks. This piece-bright paling shuts the spouse
Christ home, Christ and his mother and all his hallows.

This poem is by Gerard Manley Hopkins, a Victorian poet whose work was almost completely unknown during his life and who came to sudden fame when his collected verse was first published in 1918 and 1930. He is now reckoned to be one of the greatest poets of the century.

This poem is not by any means one of his most difficult, but it illustrates clearly enough the strong idiosyncrasy of the poet: it is a sonnet like (and how unlike!) the Shakespeare sonnet above (p. 76); here the division is firmly drawn between the first eight lines ('octave') and the last six ('sestet'), and the rhymes reinforce this division. The first eight lines are the exposition or statement, the last six the 'findings' or conclusion.

The octave invites us to look at the stars on a fine night,

starting with the plain statement, expressing wonder, "Look at the stars!" and finding a series of images to describe them in their complexity and variety. Anyone who has stared at the night sky should be able to respond. The second line with its "firefolk sitting in the air" evokes the legends of Norse peoples about stars. The third begins to see the sky itself stretching away as an ordinary terrestrial landscape does: if you look hard and long enough you begin to see, or to imagine, recessions and perspective; the brighter groups or constellations then appear as the lights of towns ("the bright boroughs") in the surrounding darkness, and a circular group can easily be seen as the centre of a town ("circle-citadels"). Behind these brighter patches are the dim immensities of further galaxies, seen as dim woods in which there are diamond mines; here by a beautiful internal echo we move from "delves," the mines of Germanic legend, to the elves who traditionally dig the diamonds, and whose eyes catch the light of the surrounding glitter.

Now the skyscape begins to open up as we stare longer and the images come flooding, all drawn by analogy from landscape. A patch of infinitely distant stars, seen only as a mist, is spattered with brighter stars, like buttercups in a lawn which is cold and grey in colour, or the early sunlight catching the grassblades: "quick-gold" is its lively glitter, "quick" meaning 'living' as in the phrase 'the quick and the dead'—not the cold glitter of the mineral diamonds but the warmer yellow tone that some stars show. The white-beam is a fine English tree the undersides of whose leaves are white, so that when it is beaten by the wind you get patches of flickering whiteness across the dull green, like the twinkle of distant stars. "Abeles" are also trees (otherwise known as white poplars), which tremble in the breeze and show the mealy white undersides of their leaves when "set on a flare"

—almost 'set alight.' The next line is a triumph of compressed vision: a sudden noise in a quiet farmyard ("a farmyard scare") sets the doves "floating forth" like flakes of snow from the dovecote in patches of shimmering white. The last line of the octave is purposely mysterious. *What* is a purchase, one asks, and what is a prize?

The sestet explains. This beauty, this richness, says the poet, is only available to him who can pay for them. with the traditional catholic 'good works' of "prayer, patience, alms, vows." At this point the beauty seems to be vanishing, and our attention, jerked from physical beauty to doctrinal abstractions, may flag; but the poet forces us, with the repeated word "look," to stare again into the sky and see what we may be losing. "Mess" means a mixture, here the blossom of an orchard in its complex beauty and its patches of light against dark, and March bloom is the pollenated surface of the willow bloom, yellow against the grey of the blossom itself (commonly called 'palm') as stars are yellow against the grey sky. This is a triumph of concentration again, with the exact word "mealed" ('dusted') to describe the way in which the surface is spattered; and "sallows," meaning a kind of willow-tree, also suggests 'grey.' "Bloom," moreover, means simultaneously 'blossom' and the powdery surface that one finds, for example on grapes or peaches. "These," meaning these beauties, however magnificent, are only the barn, inside which ("withindoors") are housed the shocks, the stored corn for which the barn is built. For a moment it seems unintelligible, until the last sentence elucidates: the sky with its patterns of stars is seen as a paling or fence, "piece-bright" (bright in pieces or patches), which hides the infinitely greater beauty and splendour of Christ in heaven ("Christ home"), the family of Christ and all the glory of the saints ("all his hallows"). It is perhaps only then that one remembers the childlike and yet deeply felt belief that heaven is in the sky, beyond the stars.

With the theological content of this poem as such we are not, of course, concerned: but the conviction of the poem transcends any particular doctrinal beliefs. The language is typical of this poet—sinewy, strong, intensely personal, intensely inventive, and it re-creates with great power the experience that brought it to birth. What might seem at first the 'oddities' of structure—the extraordinary compound adjectives ("mealed-with-yellow," "piece-bright"), the power of evocation ("the diamond delves! the elves'-eyes!" "Flakedoves"), the coinages ("withindoors," "quick-gold") the use at critical points of strong simple monosyllables ("house the shocks") and the double rhymes suggesting richness and plenitude ("sallows," "hallows") —on further examination reveal a truly individual and very personal poetry. The style has been widely, and for the most part falsely, imitated: it acts in the first place as a shock, but finishes by making much of the poetry of its period seem timid, conventional, and flabby.

(VIII)

To Autumn

Season of mists and mellow fruitfulness!
Close bosom-friend of the maturing sun;
Conspiring with him how to load and bless
With fruit the vines that round the thatch-eaves run;
To bend with apples the moss'd cottage-trees,
And fill all fruit with ripeness to the core;
To swell the gourd, and plump the hazel shells
With a sweet kernel; to set budding more,
And still more, later flowers for the bees,
Until they think warm days will never cease,
For summer has o'er-brimmed their clammy cells.

Who hath not seen thee oft amid thy store?
Sometimes whoever seeks abroad may find
Thee sitting careless on a granary floor,
Thy hair soft-lifted by the winnowing wind;
Or on a half-reap'd furrow, sound asleep,
Drows'd with the fume of poppies, while thy hook
Spares the next swath and all its twinèd flowers:
And sometimes like a gleaner thou dost keep
Steady thy laden head across a brook;
Or by a cider-press, with patient look,
Thou watchest the last oozings, hours by hours.

Where are the songs of Spring? Ay, where are they?
Think not of them, thou hast thy music too—
While barrèd clouds bloom the soft-dying day,
And touch the stubble-plains with rosy hue;
Then in a wailful choir the small gnats mourn
Among the river sallows, borne aloft
Or sinking as the light wind lives or dies;
And full-grown lambs loud bleat from hilly bourn;
Hedge-crickets sing; and now with treble soft
The red-breast whistles from a garden-croft,
And gathering swallows twitter in the skies.

This justly famous ode is one of five great odes that John Keats wrote towards the end of his short life. We find in his letters some references to walks about Winchester which he took in 1819, which offer parallels to details in this poem.

The first verse brings together in concentration what one might call the 'harvest' aspect of autumn, the second a series of sharply seen pictures of typical autumnal pursuits, and the third is mainly concerned with the sounds of autumn. Put like this, the structure of the poem sounds elementary: but the more we look at it the more subtly is it found to be balanced.

The first verse concentrates all the elements in autumn which suggest fruition, the emphasis being on internal ripeness. It is remarkable how many evocations are combined in this one verse. At the outset "mists" and "mellow" give the two contrasting elements with which the rest of the poem deals: and the rest of the verse suggests richness everywhere: one has only to look at the adjectives —"mellow," "bosom," "maturing," "sweet," "later," "warm," "clammy," and the corresponding verbs "load" "bend," "fill," "swell," "plump," "o'erbrimmed," to see how he is 'loading every rift with ore,' as he said in a letter. The accumulations of ripeness and richness in autumn, in fact, correspond to the richness of texture of the verse. The "maturing" sun is the sun which matures the fruit and also the sun which is at its ripest, before its decline. The generalized picture is given sharpness and locality by "thatch-eves," "moss'd cottage-trees," bending under the weight of fruit. (A gourd is a member of the marrow—pumpkin family of plants, whose fruits have bright coloured skins and a peculiar bulky lushness.) The verse finishes with a climax of excess in the picture of the late blossom and the bees still accumulating honey—there is almost too much ripeness in these calm autumn days. But the slightly sickly note of excess, common in Keats' early work, is here an essential part of the poem, part of the effect intended, and is cooled down, as it were, by the second and even more by the third verse.

It is interesting to note that syntactically the first verse has no main verb: this would be quite without significance except that the effect of continuity aimed at throughout, the warm autumn days going on and on—("more and still more," "warm days will never cease") is strengthened by the absence of a main verb, which would tend to close the movement. The whole of the first verse can be thought of as an address to autumn ('O you season of mists . . .') or one can say that the movement of the verse is concluded by the main verb in the opening of the second verse:

> Who hath not seen thee oft amid thy store?

The second verse consists of four sharply seen pictures—vignettes—of typical autumnal pursuits—threshing, reaping, gleaning, and cider-making. A closer look reveals that in fact none of the four figures is active: each is suspended in one way or another. The words "thee" and "thou" are gently insinuated and a full reading reveals that the peasants 'embody' the autumn that surrounds them and are thus 'versions' of the god or goddess of autumn ("may find *thee* sitting careless," "sometimes like a gleaner *thou* dost keep"). They are simultaneously agricultural workers, figures in a landscape, symbols of the autumnal activities they carry out, and incarnations of autumn itself. Though autumn is a busy period, it is also sleepy and deeply meditative. Thus the first figure who has been threshing sits careless on the granary floor, and the light wind that has been winnowing the grain blows through the open doorway and lifts his hair gently. The second has been reaping with a sickle and now lies fast asleep, in the sun. The acrid scent of crushed poppy stems surrounds him and makes him drowsy; they have been cut with the corn, and opium comes from a kind of poppy. His sickle has not yet cut the next swath—the amount that one cuts with a sweep of the sickle—and small flowers like field convolvulus are visible, twined around the stems of the standing corn. The third figure is a gleaner carrying a basket or sack of gleanings on his (her?) head, and poised half way across the stepping-stones of a brook, balancing and for the moment suspended. The last image is of the worker at the cider-press, who is standing patiently by the press watching the last trickles of juice come out—the concentrated essence of autumn. The statuesque stillness of these four figures makes the middle verse act as a sort of pivot balancing the two accumulative sensory verses on either side.

The third verse starts with a reminder of the infinitely distant spring, about which so many songs have been written. Spring is the most remote season from autumn; hence the repetition "Ay, where *are* they?" Autumn has been relatively neglected and Keats wishes to offer it the same kind of praise as is traditionally given to spring: "thou hast thy music too." The autumnal evening is beautifully and precisely evoked by "barrèd clouds," the long thin clouds of evening, "bloom," suggesting both softness and colour, and by the stubble fields after the reaping is over, touched by the pink light of the early sunset. From here to the end of the poem is a series of beautifully modulated sounds. The "wailful choir" of gnats hovering over the water mourns the passing of summer, and lifts and sinks nearer the surface as the breeze touches them; the last grasshoppers sing in the grass; the robin, a typical symbol of winter, comes closer to man and its thin song is heard again now that the other birds are silent; and finally there is the chatter of migrating swallows, excited and yet poignant for us, gathering into flocks for their journey southwards and leaving us alone to face the winter.

The images in the last verse balance the richness and warmth of the first stanza in a number of ways: they evoke the evening rather than midday, and it is the autumnal evening which pre-eminently brings the first notes of winter; they describe thin aural images instead of rich visual and tactile ones; and they disentangle from the total experience of autumn those elements which look beyond to winter, just as the first stanza 'sees' autumn as the fulfilment of summer. One can say therefore that the first and last stanzas give together what is unique and particular about autumn, a bridge between summer and winter, with the chilly elements gradually dominating and overtaking the remnants of summer.

The beauty of the individual lines of this ode has been often enough noted, but it is as a triumph of 'organization' that it stands supreme. The strongly contrasted outside verses are held together by the calm classical stillness of the middle verse, and the structure seems inevitable as it does only in the greatest poetry.

Chapter Five

SOME PASSAGES FROM DRAMA EXAMINED

(I)

These are the forgeries of jealousy:
And never, since the middle summer's spring,
Met we on hill, in dale, forest, or mead,
By pavèd fountain or by rushy brook,
Or in the beachèd margent of the sea,
To dance our ringlets to the whistling wind,
But with thy brawls thou hast disturb'd our sport.
Therefore the winds, piping to us in vain,
As in revenge, have suck'd up from the sea
Contagious fogs; which falling in the land
Have every pelting river made so proud
That they have overborne their continents:
The ox hath therefore stretched his yoke in vain,
The ploughman lost his sweat; and the green corn
Hath rotted ere his youth attain'd a beard:
The fold stands empty in the drownèd field,
And crows are fatted with the murrion flock;
The nine men's morris is fill'd up with mud,
And the quaint mazes in the wanton green,
For lack of tread are undistinguishable;
The human mortals want their winter here;
No night is now with hymn or carol blest:—
Therefore the moon, the governess of floods,
Pale in her anger, washes all the air,
That rheumatic diseases do abound:
And thorough this distemperature we see
The seasons alter; hoary-headed frosts

Fall in the fresh lap of the crimson rose;
And on old Hiems' thin and icy crown
An odorous chaplet of sweet summer buds
Is, as in mockery, set: the spring, the summer,
The childing autumn, angry winter, change
Their wonted liveries, and the mazèd world,
By their increase, now knows not which is which:
And this same progeny of evils comes
From our debate, from our dissension;
We are their parents and original.

WILLIAM SHAKESPEARE: from
A Midsummer Night's Dream

OBERON and Titania, king and queen of fairyland, have quarrelled about a changeling child whom they both want in their retinue. They make various accusations about one another, and the climax is the long speech of Titania, in which the disturbance in nature is blamed on the fairies' quarrel.

The general drift of Titania's speech does not need any very detailed analysis; but a little 'background' is needed to understand the way in which the main ideas work. It was a common belief from Greek times, and indeed in many 'primitive' religions, that disturbances among the gods are echoed in disturbances on earth, and also that the behaviour of nature echoes the behaviour of the great among men (kings, for example, are divine figures). For the purposes of this passage we are made to believe that the continuity of the seasonal pattern depends on amity among supernatural beings, and that such a quarrel as that between Titania and Oberon will result in the normal seasonal process going awry. To put it more simply, brawls in nature derive from brawls among the fairies: nature is no longer governed and controlled. Whenever Titania and her train have met for their usual pastimes and pursuits (which seem purposeless 'fun' but have the function of keeping nature itself on an even keel), Oberon has spoiled the occasion ("With thy brawls thou hast disturbed our sport"). The two words "Therefore" introduce the disasters that have followed, and the description continues until three lines from the end ("now knows not which is which"). The speech ends with the firm statement that all this chaos comes from the fairies' quarrel.

Titania's speech opens with a dignified reply to Oberon's accusations about her love affairs with mortals ("These are the forgeries of jealousy"). The "middle summer's spring," an odd expression to a modern ear, means simply the beginning of midsummer. The next few lines show an elaboration and proliferation common in Shakespeare's earlier work: the detail is not organic or structural, but decorative. "Hill," "dale," "fountain," "brook," "sea-shore," these are variations for their own sake—though one could probably add that they do reinforce the idea that the fairies are present in all of nature and inhabit all possible scenic contexts. "Ringlets" are the fairy-rings seen on certain pasture fields and then supposed to be made by the fairies' round-dances. The winds, no longer governed by the fairies' will, have brought up sea fogs which in turn have made every pelting ('paltry') river so much fuller and faster-flowing than usual ("proud") that they have over-flowed their banks ("overborne their continents"). This flooding has spoiled the labours of the peasantry; the ox, straining against the wooden yoke on his neck as he pulls the plough, has worked in vain, the ploughman has wasted his hard work ("lost his sweat"), and the young corn has rotted in the wet fields before it reached maturity; the long hairs on the mature ears of wheat or barley are thought of as a beard, and the line finely suggests the pathos of the young corn dying before reaching even the symbol of being adult, which in Elizabethan times was of course the growing of a beard. The sheepfold is empty in the waterlogged field and the crows gorge themselves on the diseased bodies of the sheep ("murrion flock"). Nor is the effect felt only by 'nature' or agriculture. The nine men's morris is a game played on a series of squares cut out from the turf in grass; now it is filled up with mud and the game cannot be played. So also the "quaint mazes" or labyrinths and patterns on the village green ("wanton" here means given over to sports and pastimes) are neglected and therefore invisible. Human beings lack ("want") the ordinary activities of winter evenings, because there is no real winter or summer. The hymns and carols associated with winter festivals are no longer sung because the whole basis of peasant life, in both its agricultural and its leisure aspects, has collapsed with the collapse of the very pattern of seasonal change and growth that brought it into being.

The second "therefore" echoes the first one, which dealt with the wind and the subsequent floodings, and both are dependent on the line

> . . . With thy brawls thou hast disturbed our sport.

The moon controls the weather and governs the floods; she is pale with anger and brings dampness and a series of complaints like colds and aches ("rheumatic" has a stress on the first syllable and covers a wide range of illnesses). Through ("thorough") this lack of temperance or moderation ("distemperature") the seasons themselves go wrong: frosts, personified as white-haired ("hoary-headed"), destroy the roses of June; and on the icy crown of Hiems, the god of winter, a sweet-smelling crown of summer flowers is set as if in mockery. Late frosts, in fact, ruin the summer flowers, while unusually mild damp weather in the winter brings forth flowers out of season. The four seasons ("childing" means 'prolific') change their usual costumes ("wonted liveries") and the confused and astonished ("mazèd") world can no longer distinguish them. These evil offspring ("progeny of evils") result from our quarrel: we are their parents, and they derive from us.

This is a beautifully sustained passage and its virtues lie in its lyrical charm and the rich elaboration of its detail. Its rhythms are contained in a fairly rigid five-stress line which tends to be a unit and only occasionally flows on to the next line, though within this pattern some very delicate rhythmic variations occur. It has relatively little dramatic purpose, and has the character of a rhetorical set-piece which does little to move the situation forward or give any insight into the personality of Titania, if indeed she is to be thought to have one at all. Compared with the more mature work of Shakespeare (see the passages from *Macbeth* and *Antony*) it seems static, and, in spite of its unquestionable beauty and delicacy, to be a piece of lavish description for its own sake, the kind of writing that might be expected from an exceptionally gifted and sensitive young poet still remembering his country childhood. It has perhaps a remote dramatic function in that, when Titania and Oberon are at length reconciled, peace and stability return to the world; but within the pattern of this section of the play it is dismissed immediately and never referred to again.

(II)

LORD CHIEF JUSTICE. Are you not ashamed to enforce a poor widow to so rough a course to come by her own?

FALSTAFF. What is the gross sum that I owe thee?

HOSTESS. Marry, if thou wert an honest man, thyself and the money too. Thou didst swear to me upon a parcel-gilt goblet, sitting in my Dolphin-chamber, at the round table, by a sea-coal fire, upon Wednesday in Wheeson-week, when the Prince broke thy head for liking his father to a singing-man of Windsor—thou didst swear to me then, as I was washing thy wound, to marry me, and make me my lady thy wife. Canst thou deny it? Did not goodwife Keech, the butcher's wife, come in then, and call me gossip Quickly? coming in to borrow a mess of vinegar; telling us she had a good dish of prawns; whereby thou didst desire to eat some; whereby I told thee they were ill for a green wound? And didst thou not, when she was gone down stairs, desire me to be no more so familiarity with such poor people; saying that ere long they should call me madam? And didst thou not kiss me, and bid me fetch thee thirty shillings? I put thee now to thy book-oath: deny it, if thou canst.

FALSTAFF. My lord, this is a poor mad soul; and she says, up and down the town, that her eldest son is like you; she hath been in good case, and the truth is, poverty hath distracted her.

WILLIAM SHAKESPEARE:
from *Henry IV Part II*

Mistress Quickly, hostess of the Boar's Head Tavern in Eastcheap, London, has had Sir John Falstaff arrested for debt to her; he is denying all her accusations to the Lord Chief Justice, and the Hostess is explaining that Falstaff not only owes her money but has promised to marry her.

Before this passage opens the Lord Chief Justice asks for what sum Falstaff has been arrested, and the Hostess replies, "It is more than for some, my lord; it is for all—all I have."

Falstaff's gruff question "What is the gross sum that I owe thee?" is asked in the knowledge that she has lost count. Hence she changes her ground and claims that he owes her "thyself and the money too." She then goes on to give a circumstantial account of the occasion when Falstaff has promised to marry her; it is evident from her account, though she appears not to realize it herself, that he has only been leading up to an attempt to borrow more money ("Didst thou not kiss me, and bid me fetch thee thirty shillings?").

Some notes on the details of the speech may be found helpful. "Parcel-gilt" means partly gilt, or gilded; the goblet was presumably the one he was drinking from at the time. "Dolphin-chamber" illustrates the practice of naming rooms in taverns, common at the time and not unknown now. The hostess's detail gets more and more meticulous—what he swore on, which room they were sitting in, where in the room, how warmed ("sea coal" is coal brought by sea, probably from the north-east coast), on what day—it is typical of her that she remembers the day and the week. "Wheeson" is a colloquial if not illiterate version of Whitsun (elsewhere she refers to Pistol as "Peesel"). The prince is of course Prince Hal, the heir to the throne, who is living the life of a wastrel with Falstaff, but obviously draws the line somewhere, and has just given Falstaff a scalp-wound for insulting the King his father. When she is washing Falstaff's wound he promises to make her "*my* lady thy wife." The "my" is rather delightful, and suggests that the hostess has only thought of ladies as people to address politely and remotely, with a curtsey as it were: moreover she envisages herself in the future as being addressed thus by those who at present are her social equals. "Canst thou deny it?" gives Falstaff no chance to answer and the 'squawky' note in her voice increases as she moves from statement (the elaborate sentence in the first half) to a series of rhetorical questions in a rising crescendo. "Goodwife" is a common expression for a citizen's wife, and she refers to the Hostess as "gossip" Quickly, which then simply meant an old or middle-aged woman—it patronizes mildly but does not abuse: the dramatic point is that the appellation shows the two women to be familiar and on equal terms. It contrasts with her ambition to be "my lady thy wife", and stimulates Falstaff's careful exploitation of her snobbery in desiring her to be "no more so familiarity with such poor people." The vinegar dressing is for a dish of prawns which the hostess, perhaps in her new rôle as wife-designate, denies Falstaff on the grounds that they are bad for a fresh ("green") wound. "Ere long they should call me madam" repeats "my lady thy wife," and stresses her naive but rooted snobbery, and the irony lies in her having much more money than Falstaff, who could give her a title but would exploit her financially if ever he married her, and meanwhile uses his promises to get more money out of her.

The speech ends with a triumphant 'squawk' ("book-oath" is an oath on the Bible) and the whole effect is of a righteous indignation rising to a climax as she remembers the full details, breaking off only when she runs out of breath. Falstaff's voice is heavy, slow, would-be dignified ('we men have seen this sort of thing before, especially from women'): his deliberation and his bass voice must contrast with the indignant screeching of the hostess just as physically his bulk and stature contrast with her smallness.

This is a passage typical of the prose found in the mature history plays—a strong muscular prose, rich in detail, forceful in rhythm and full of 'local colour'—here indeed the statement of the hostess is so weighed down with local colour that the narrative thread is lost. The rhythms and diction of the speech are themselves a character-sketch o the speaker. She is shrewd in some ways, yet opinionated, illiterate and naive, extremely voluble and unable to reach her point without a wealth of irrelevant detail, through which one sees that this is her mode of remembering things and at the same time a means of convincing her listeners that her statements are true ('No one could invent all this'). She can grasp things only in the order in which they occurred and cannot separate them from a mass of irrelevancies. Her life is cluttered with—indeed, it almost consists of—a mass of domestic detail and gossip with other housewives, all remembered with enormous relish. This kind of monologue is produced with remarkable fidelity and authenticity and gives the whole passage a contemporary air; a conversation in a bus-queue or a talk over a garden fence nowadays can be exactly like this except in the particularity of its detail. Falstaff can't get a word in during the flood, but answers at the end in the hope that her incoherent indignation can be passed off as madness. He adds an oblique insult to the Lord Chief Justice ("she says up and down the town, that her eldest son is like you") with the intention of distracting him from the matter in hand, hinting that publicity would be unwise—or alternately implying that *nothing* she says is to be trusted—'she is an incorrigible gossip'—and in general hoping to confuse the trail.

(III)

ROSS. When I came hither to transport the tidings,
Which I have heavily borne, there ran a rumour
Of many worthy fellows that were out;
Which was to my belief witness'd the rather,
For that I saw the tyrant's power afoot:

Now is the time of help; your eye in Scotland
Would create soldiers, make our women fight,
To doff their dire distresses.

MALCOLM. Be't their comfort
We are coming thither: gracious England hath
Lent us good Siward and ten thousand men;
An older and a better soldier none
That Christendom gives out.

ROSS. Would I could answer
This comfort with the like! But I have words
That would be howl'd out in the desert air,
Where hearing should not latch them.

MACDUFF. What concern they?
The general cause? or is it a fee-grief
Due to some single breast?

ROSS. No man that's honest
But in it shares some woe, though the main part
Pertains to you alone.

MACDUFF. If it be mine,
Keep it not from me, quickly let me have it.

ROSS. Let not your ears despise my tongue for ever,
Which shall possess them with the heaviest sound
That ever yet they heard.

MACDUFF. Hum! I guess at it.

ROSS. Your castle is surpris'd; your wife and babes
Savagely slaughter'd: to relate the manner,
Were, on the quarry of these murder'd deer,
To add the death of you.

MALCOLM. Merciful heaven!—
What, man! ne'er pull your hat upon your brows;
Give sorrow words: the grief that does not speak
Whispers the o'er-fraught heart, and bids it break.

MACDUFF. My children too?

ROSS. Wife, children, servants, all
That could be found.

MACDUFF. And I must be from thence!—
My wife kill'd too?

ROSS. I have said.

MALCOLM. Be comforted:
Let's make us medicines of our great revenge,
To cure this deadly grief.

MACDUFF. He has no children.—All my pretty ones?
Did you say all?—O hell-kite!—All?
What, all my pretty chickens and their dam
At one fell swoop?

MALCOLM. Dispute it like a man.

MACDUFF. I shall do so;
But I must also feel it as a man:
I cannot but remember such things were,
That were most precious to me.

WILLIAM SHAKESPEARE:
from *Macbeth*

Macbeth, king of Scotland, having killed the rightful king, is ruling the country as a bloody tyrant. Macduff, a leading noble, has recently escaped to England to join the rebel forces led by young Malcolm, legitimate heir to the throne. Ross now arrives with the latest news from Scotland and advocates an iinmediate invasion; but he must also break to Macduff the news that Macbeth has sacked his castle and slaughtered his wife and family.

Ross brings an appalling picture of the situation in Scotland where "good men's lives Expire before the flowers in their caps." His opening speech here is quoted only as introduction to what follows: many worthy fellows are "out," that is, out in open rebellion, and this is confirmed by the "tyrant's power" being "afoot"—that is, Macbeth's own army is in the field. If Malcolm were now to invade, every one would join him, even the women. The young Malcolm gives a confident answer and mentions the support that England has given. Ross wishes that he had equally comforting news to offer—

> But I have words
> That would be howled out in the desert air,
> Where hearing should not latch them.

So dreadful is his news that it is fit only to be howled in a deserted place where no one could hear it, take it in through his ear, and make it his as one closes a door and takes possession of a room. Macduff asks whether this news is tragic for "the general cause" or for some particular person. Ross says that every good man will be appalled by the news but it is mainly for Macduff only. Macduff begs to know it quickly. Ross prays that he may not be despised for ever for bringing such news. Macduff by this time has guessed the truth. Ross tells him flatly that his family is dead and that he cannot describe the manner of their deaths or the shock would kill Macduff as well, and add his body to the "quarry" or pile of innocent corpses ("deer"). Macduff cannot speak and Malcolm intervenes to say that he must. Macduff cannot believe the truth and repeats the questions again and again. Malcolm advocates a spirit of revenge but Macduff hardly hears him: he shows bewilderment and a tender love for his lost family.

Such a paraphrase can only offer the lightest sketch of what is actually given here. The full dramatic intensity cannot, of course, be felt without reading the whole scene and indeed the whole play. But there is enough here to show the subtle interplay of the three speakers. Ross is horrified at his own task, and imagines, as we all would in such circumstances, that he can perhaps find some means of breaking the news gently. But that, inevitably, is impossible;

no euphemisms can soften the intrinsic horror of the revelation, and in the end he must force himself to say it flatly and almost as savagely as it happened, and to recognize how hopeless it is to try to soften its impact. This is shown also by his further 'flat' answers ("Wife, children, servants, all That could be found" and "I have said"). Malcolm is young and uncomprehending, and though his first intervention ("Merciful heaven. . . .") is meant to relieve the pressure on Macduff's mind ("What man, ne'er pull your hat upon your brows . . ."), his second attempt to comfort him ("Let's make us medicines of our great revenge . . .") is clumsy and brash, and his third ("Dispute it like a man") goes near to suggesting that Macduff's grief is undignified if not effeminate. Macduff's magnificent answer 'places' Malcolm and himself superbly: his family is now hideously seen in retrospect ("such things *were*, That *were* most precious to me") and he defines how a mature man *must* feel about such a disaster, and makes Malcolm's implied definition of a 'man' (in "Dispute it like a man") callow and adolescent in comparison. Macduff's bewilderment and incredulity is shown by his silence, and his repeated questions imply that he cannot take in the enormity of the news but can only accept it piecemeal: "My wife killed *too*?" (as well as my children) "My children *too*?" (as well as my wife). At last his anguish and fury come through:

> O hell-kite!—All?
> What, all my pretty chickens and their dam
> At one fell swoop?

Here Lady Macduff and her children are the innocent 'domesticated' fowls, and Macbeth the savage hawk swooping down on them. The word "all," which he cannot absorb, is at last embraced by his imagination. He has at last "latched" the words that should have been "howl'd out in the desert air."

There is a great deal more for discussion in this passage, but it has been used here mainly to show how Shakespeare can represent a whole pattern of personal inter-relations in a remarkably economical way. Seldom has the anguish of such a loss been more exactly rendered.

(IV)

(*Enter* DEMETRIUS *and* PHILO.

PHILO. Nay, but this dotage of our general's
O'erflows the measure: those his goodly eyes
That o'er the files and musters of the war
Have glow'd like plated Mars, now bend, now turn,
The office and devotion of their view
Upon a tawny front: his captain's heart
Which in the scuffles of great fights hath burst
The buckles on his breast, reneges all temper,
And is become the bellows and the fan
To cool a gipsy's lust. (*Flourish within.*) Look where they come:
Take but good note, and you shall see in him
The triple pillar of the world transform'd
Into a strumpet's fool: behold and see.

Enter ANTONY, CLEOPATRA, *her* LADIES, *the* TRAIN, *with* EUNUCHS *fanning her.*

CLEOPATRA. If it be love indeed, tell me how much.
ANTONY. There's beggary in the love that can be reckon'd.
CLEOPATRA. I'll set a bourn how far to be belov'd.
ANTONY. Then must thou needs find out new heaven, new earth.

(*Enter an* ATTENDANT.

ATTENDANT. News, my good lord, from Rome.
ANTONY. Grates me:—the sum.

CLEOPATRA. Nay, hear them, Antony:
Fulvia perchance is angry; or, who knows
If the scarce-bearded Caesar have not sent
His powerful mandate to you, 'Do this, or this;
Take in that kingdom, and enfranchise that;
Perform't, or else we damn thee.'

WILLIAM SHAKESPEARE:
from *Antony and Cleopatra*

This is part of the opening scene of the play. It takes place in a room in Cleopatra's palace in Alexandria. Demetrius and Philo are two "friends of Antony," lieutenants in his army.

Philo's opening speech summarizes the attitude of the professional soldier to Antony's love-affair with Cleopatra. He is in the middle of a conversation with Demetrius, hence "nay"; the word "dotage" carries the meaning of passionate fondness as well as feeble-mindedness, and it "o'erflows the measure" in the sense that it exceeds all proper bounds. Antony's eyes, that used to glow like "plated Mars" (Mars' eyes or the glitter of his armour) on his troops, now "bend" (lower themselves) and "turn" (as if following Cleopatra's every movement) from their proper duties and devotion, those of a soldier, to a dark-skinned face ("front" is literally 'forehead'). His heart, once so powerful and courageous in hand-to-hand fighting as to burst the buckles of his breastplate—the muscular image is that of a panting warrior and not merely a military leader—now forgoes all moderation ("reneges all temper"), and is reduced from its previous glory to a humble instrument for pacifying the appetites of a gipsy ("gipsy," for Cleopatra, is originally short for 'Egyptian': here it is contemptuous in the extreme). Philo has already stirred the audience to the strongest curiosity about the lovers when a flourish on the trumpets warns of their approach, and the reflective note in his speech gives way to indignant immediacy. Demetrius can see for himself whether Philo is exaggerating; if he watches them closely he will see one of the three pillars of the world (Antony is governing the Roman Empire in a triumvirate with Octavius Caesar and Lepidus) turned into a slave and clown serving a harlot ("fool" is 'lickspittle servant' as well as 'plaything' and 'court-jester'). On "Behold, and see", the audience's expectation identifies itself with that of Demetrius.

Antony and Cleopatra then enter majestically, with her splendid train of attendants and eunuchs following her, and they, too, are in the middle of a dialogue. Cleopatra asks how much he loves her, if indeed it *is* love, and Antony replies that a love which can be measured is beggary in comparison with his. Cleopatra says she will set a limit to his love, and he answers that no limit can be set on this earth. The dialogue, gentle, amused, playing amiably with phrases and yet carrying strong undertones of passion, contrasts in its intimacy with the 'public' critical voice of Philo and the voice of duty in the messenger. When the latter rushes in with what may well be vital news from Rome, Antony is transformed in a moment to the lordly despot whose private affairs are being interrupted by 'merely' political matters. He is brusque and irritated: 'it vexes me: give me the summary, be brief' ("Grates me: —the sum"). Before the attendant can answer, Cleopatra protests sarcastically that the news may be important: perhaps Fulvia his wife is angry, or Octavius, who is young and callow in comparison with Antony ("the scarce-bearded Caesar"), may have instructions about new military campaigns for Antony, which, she implies, it would be dangerous to disobey. The force of her intervention is that while she pretends to ask Antony to give full attention to the messenger, she really confirms him in his conviction that nothing but their love matters, and forces him to be indifferent, under penalty of seeming either henpecked or in fear of orders from a mere boy.

The language here is as rich as the dramatic crossplay: indeed, the two aspects are inseparable. Philo's wish to draw a picture of degradation turns almost to its opposite. "Dotage," a key idea for the whole play, defines one criticism of Antony's behaviour and is beautifully confirmed by his opening dialogue with Cleopatra: yet the splendour and conviction of his love transcends this definition and makes it seem one-sided if not positively priggish. "O'erflows the measure" carries the suggestion of generosity in an over-full libation of wine as well as mere excess. In illustrating the general assertion "this dotage o'erflows the measure" the speech describes three aspects. First, "Those his goodly eyes," symbolizing his attention or activities, are now reduced to a doting stare at Cleopatra's beauty. Then, in ascending order, "his heart" (his feelings) has now become "the bellows and the fan," mere instruments for her service—the metaphor beautifully suggests stimulating appetite as well as fulfilling it, since bellows make the heat glow while the fan cools; after "scuffles" and "buckles" the movement falls to the contemptuous monosyllables "fan," "cool," "lust." The degradation implicit in "gipsy's lust" is immediately followed by the stage direction "Flourish within," the trumpet sound giving the contrasting majesty and splendour, and heralding in sound the still more splendid actual arrival of the lovers. Thirdly and finally the speech moves to its climax with "the triple pillar of the world," the whole man in his political greatness. These three terms correspond to the three phrases "upon a tawny front" (unworthy preoccupations), "to cool a gipsy's lust" (unworthy actions), and "into a strumpet's fool" (unworthy rôle), which are also on an ascending scale of importance, and correspond with one another in sentence structure and in their position within the blank verse line. The whole speech manages to imply what indeed the whole play implies, that Antony's behaviour, however much of a decline it is from one point of view, is a triumphant advance from another.

The lovers' brief dialogue, intimate and tender, does indeed illustrate the depth of Antony's "dotage": yet "new heaven, new earth" gives one a sense of the unlimited range of their love, against which the arrival of the attendant, symbolizing Antony's other life as a great Roman statesman, is made to seem constricting and irrelevant. "Grates me: the sum" shows *his* contempt for anything outside his love, and Cleopatra's sarcasm not only endorses this but almost makes the great world outside them seem objectively worthless. "Do this, or this; Take in that kingdom, and enfranchise that" makes the ambitions of statesmanship appear as futile and mechanical as a child's game. What is "Rome," or even "that kingdom, and . . . that" really worth, in comparison with "new heaven, new earth"?

The tonal and rhythmic contrasts in this brilliant opening reinforce the themes. Antony in Philo's eyes is a great world figure reduced to the plaything of a worthless love: but already by the end of the passage quoted we are aware that his love is a real competitor to his other self, and though it may indeed be "dotage" ("if it be love," says Cleopatra), it is also already established as a triumph. The themes of the whole play are stated in these lines: the rest of the play is (in a sense) a working out of what is realized here; and the stronger and more definitive the condemnation in Philo's speech the more triumphantly the love of Antony stands up against it. The swift movement throughout is typical of the whole play, and it is extraordinary how much sense of huge events is implied here. The vigour of the opening speech, the disembodied contemplative dialogue of the lovers, the urgency of the messenger, the brusque irritation of Antony, the stinging irony of Cleopatra, all contribute to a sense of actuality and a glowing splendour. This passage shows our greatest dramatist at the very height of his powers.

(V)

PERDITA. O, these I lack
To make you garlands of; and my sweet friend,
To strew him o'er and o'er!
FLORIZEL. What, like a corse?
PERDITA. No, like a bank for love to lie and play on;
Not like a corse; or if,—not to be buried,
But quick, and in mine arms. Come, take your flowers:
Methinks I play as I have seen them do
In Whitsun pastorals: sure, this robe of mine
Does change my disposition.
FLORIZEL. What you do
Still betters what is done. When you speak, sweet,
I'ld have you do it ever: when you sing,
I'ld have you buy and sell so; so give alms;
Pray so; and, for the ord'ring your affairs,
To sing them too: when you do dance, I wish you
A wave o' the sea, that you might ever do
Nothing but that; move still, still so,
And own no other function: each your doing,
So singular in each particular,
Crowns what you are doing in the present deeds,
That all your acts are queens.
PERDITA. O Doricles,
Your praises are too large: but that your youth,

And the true blood which peeps fairly through't,
Do plainly give you out an unstain'd shepherd,
With wisdom I might fear, my Doricles,
You woo'd me the false way.

FLORIZEL. I think you have
As little skill to fear as I have purpose
To put you to't. But, come; our dance, I pray:
Your hand, my Perdita: so turtles pair,
That never mean to part.

PERDITA. I'll swear for 'em.

POLIXENES. This is the prettiest low-born lass that ever
Ran on the green-sward: nothing she does or seems
But smacks of something greater than herself,
Too noble for this place.

CAMILLO. He tells her something
That makes her blood look out: good sooth, she is
The queen of curds and cream.

WILLIAM SHAKESPEARE:
from *The Winter's Tale*

Perdita, who believes herself a shepherd's daughter, but who is really a princess, is dressed as the goddess Flora and acting as hostess at a sheep-shearing festival in pastoral Bohemia. One of her duties is to give appropriate flowers and herbs as gifts to her guests. Florizel is Polixenes' son disguised as a peasant, and is in love with Perdita. Polixenes is present disguised as a shepherd, with Camillo his counsellor.

The Winter's Tale is one of Shakespeare's latest plays, and until fairly recently was rather despised by many critics for its unreality. Some commentators even described it as the work of a tired and exhausted dramatist. It is now recognized as a major play and one of his greatest achievements. The extract given comes from the magnificent pastoral scene, which ought to be read in full, even if there is not time to study the whole play.

Perdita's speech about the flowers of spring is justly famous; she expresses a wish that she had spring flowers to give her guests, but because of the season she has only the flowers of middle summer. What follows has been perhaps less often examined. Throughout the passage we need to be aware that she is in fact of royal blood, so that not only is she distinguished from the peasant girls around her—a relatively simple observation like the proverb 'blood will out'—but she is also a perfect representative of them. In the robes of Flora, the goddess of nature, which she wears in this scene, there is implied a sort of equation: peasant girl=princess=goddess. Her innate modesty pulls against the kind of assumed boldness which her rôle as hostess necessitates and her robes provide; and she is at once proud of her achievement since it is 'out of character' and ashamed at what may appear immodest. At the outset, having described such spring flowers as daffodils, violets, primroses, oxlips, lilacs, and roses, and paid compliments to all the younger people ("O these I lack To make *you* garlands of" —that is, all of you), she selects Florizel (whom she knows as Doricles) as the chief person she is thinking of. His beauty and her love for him need the strewn flowers. Florizel's "What, like a corse?" refers to the practice of scattering blossoms at the corpse in the grave, and is made aside to Perdita. It brings out her bold and beautiful answer with its repeated negatives denying death and asserting the fullness of life and love; "but quick" has a sharp light movement, and is followed by a pause before "and in my arms," which makes "quick" suggest 'lively' and 'passionate' as well as merely 'living.' She gives the flowers from her basket to the other merry-makers ("Come, take your flowers") and expresses her own surprise at her rôle as an actress by comparing it with the freedom of the actors in the Whitsun pastorals, which she must have half envied and half deplored. The robe, and the part it involves, seem to have transformed her nature. Half her task is mere hospitality, half a symbolic rôle in a rite which has echoes of fertility ceremonials. Earlier she was blamed by her 'father,' an old peasant, for being too shy and retiring as hostess: now that she is playing the part properly she retires in embarrassment even as she advances in boldness.

Florizel's answer is worth deep study. The language is astonishingly simple and the meaning inexhaustibly profound. In essence he is praising Perdita for being herself. Whatever she *does* seems flawless to him. The repetition of the word "do" and its compounds throughout the speech is of the greatest importance. On the face of it this is a characterless little word, which represents in such general terms the carrying out of almost any action that it has no colour of its own: but as used here it is made to carry great depth of meaning. At the outset he praises all her actions, her being: "What you do" (which means 'whatever you do') "betters what is done" in the sense that it extends the possibilities of what can be done or has ever been done. The crude players in the Whitsun pastorals are put in their place for ever in these lines. When she speaks, he wishes her to go on for ever; and when, even better, she sings, he wishes that all her acts could be conducted in song—activities as commonplace and everyday as buying and selling, as ennobling and selfless as giving alms, as holy and sacrosanct as praying; and as for the "ordering your affairs," all processes of ordinary living, they too should be expressed in song. When she dances, he wishes her to be a wave on the seashore, so that she could go on for ever as a wave does. "Move still, still so" carries beautifully the rise, the momentary pause on "still" and the comma, and the backward flow on "so"; and when one remembers that "still" means 'always' as well as carrying a hint of the stillness when the crest of the wave pauses before it breaks, one sees that the concept involves a paradox of perpetual stillness and perpetual motion. Florizel pictures her poised for ever in a momentary pose which embodies and implies the movement before and after, as a statue is still but can imply movement in its very lines. When she dances she should "own no other function," that is, perform no other act. He summarizes after "function" by saying that every act of hers, so unique, personal, individual, seems to express and glorify her essence ("crowns what you are doing") in whatever she is doing now ("in the present deeds"), so that every one of her acts seem more perfect than any before ("all your acts are queens"). At the end of the speech there is a system of correspondences ("function" is echoed by "doing," "singular" by "particular," and "crowns" by "queens"). Not only are her acts 'queenly' but they are themselves "queens," of outstanding beauty, dignity, and rightness.

The speech can now be seen to have a developing movement from "speak," which seems perfect while she speaks, to "sing," which embodies more of the personality (including speaking, as it were, but embodying a new dimension), and then "dance," which involves an expression of the total personality, the body and the spirit.[1] Each is for Florizel perfect and each is transcended by the next. The speech is 'crowned' by the images of regality at its end, and one can without over-elaborating disentangle these meanings: she is only a peasant, but of so unique and beautiful a kind that everything she does seems royal; she is dressed as a goddess

[1] Hopkins' sonnet *Kingfishers catch fire* and the last verse of Yeats' *Among Schoolchildren*, though they both present considerable difficulties, express a similar concept.

and indeed seems and behaves like one; she is in fact a princess, and "crowns" and "queens" reminds the audience of this; she will in fact be a queen, since Florizel, a prince, intends to marry her; she ennobles her surroundings and the peasants she 'represents'; and behind the whole, she is a girl who expresses in every word, note, gesture, or movement, her own essence, which dignifies, ennobles, and "crowns" her personality both as an individual and as representative of young womanhood in general.

Perdita's reply is modest: "Your praises are too large" means that they are excessive, that she doesn't deserve them. Indeed if it were not that his manifest youthfulness and his blushing as he speaks show him manifestly ("give you out") to be an innocent, honest, and sincere youth, she might with some justification believe ("with wisdom I might fear") that he was flattering her insincerely in order to win her love. "The true blood" suggests the glow on his cheeks, the sincerity and modesty under his assumed boldness, and more remotely, the true blood of the prince under the guise of the shepherd. "Shepherd" is simply her name for 'man' here—they are all shepherds: the irony is in the fact that he is only disguised as one. Florizel's reply assures her of what she already knows, that she has no need to fear an intention which is impossible for him. He invites her to dance, and taking her hand, compares the two of them to turtle-doves, which symbolize constancy. As they start the movement of the dance they are observed by Polixenes and Camillo, whose comments are, as it were, on behalf of the audience, since they form a stage audience for the dance. Polixenes is aware of some special quality in her. Everything she "does" (this reminds us of Florizel's rich use of the word), or "seems" (Polixenes' caution, since she can surely only 'seem' as noble as she appears) offers a taste of ("smacks of") qualities which he would not expect among the humble peasantry. Camillo cannot hear what the lovers are saying but sees that Florizel has made her blush: "makes her blood look out" means mainly that she blushes (and echoes her own earlier remark to Florizel about his "true blood which fairly peeps through") but also faintly suggests her noble blood, and beautifully contrasts with the pale tones of "The queen of curds and cream," which simply means 'a queen among shepherdesses.' The word "queen" is again significant, and like Perdita's own beauty and bearing, means more than is apparent on the surface.

This ends one of the most magnificent modulations in Shakespeare. It would be possible to add a great deal by way of general comment or implication, and a few pointers for further discussion may be suggested here. There is a superb poise throughout between the claims and qualities of the peasantry, which are always dignified but never sentimentalized, and those of the nobility, which are shown to be somehow real and yet exclusive and self-centred. The dramatic needs—though this is not mainly a play of character—are amply fulfilled, and one way of looking at Florizel's central speech here is to say simply that it is an elaborate compliment to Perdita, the speech of an entranced lover. Polixenes and Camillo are likely on the whole to be resistant to Perdita's charms and therefore relatively remote from the intensities of love, while their nobility makes them prone to despise the brutal peasantry; yet they are drawn into the circle of her enchantment, and this intensifies our own conviction of her beauty and uniqueness. Throughout this scene Shakespeare is drawing not only upon an unparalleled knowledge and insight into human emotion, but also upon a complex background of peasant culture, a real folk culture which has almost vanished, at any rate in this country. When, later in the scene, Polixenes is to attack his son Florizel savagely for daring to love a peasant girl,

Florizel sustains his position and shows willingness to forgo the throne for her love: and a further dimension is added to our appreciation by the knowledge that she is a King's daughter anyway, but would be worthy of his love whether she were or not. The changes are rung on the peasant-noble theme with great delicacy; and the fairy-tale atmosphere which in a sense surrounds the whole play and which the title itself prompts does not preclude but in fact encourages a remarkable fidelity to the realities of life.

Chapter Six

SOME PROSE PASSAGES EXAMINED

(I)

WHILST the two girls waited, Gerald Crich trotted up on a red Arab mare. He rode well and softly, pleased with the delicate quivering of the creature between his knees. And he was very picturesque, at least in Gudrun's eyes, sitting soft and close on the slender red mare, whose long tail flowed on the air. He saluted the two girls, and drew up at the crossing to wait for the gate, looking down the railway for the approaching train. In spite of her ironic smile at his picturesqueness, Gudrun liked to look at him. He was well-set and easy, his face with its warm tan showed up his whitish, coarse moustache, and his blue eyes were full of sharp light as he watched the distance.

The locomotive chuffed slowly between the banks, hidden. The mare did not like it. She began to wince away, as if hurt by the unknown noise. But Gerald pulled her back and held her head to the gate. The sharp blasts of the chuffing engine broke with more and more force on her. The repeated sharp blows of unknown, terrifying noise struck through her till she was rocking with terror. She recoiled like a spring let go. But a glistening, half-smiling look came into Gerald's face. He brought her back again, inevitably.

The noise was released, the little locomotive with her clanking steel connecting-rod emerged on the highroad, clanking sharply. The mare rebounded like a drop of water from hot iron. Ursula and Gudrun pressed back into the hedge, in fear. But Gerald was heavy on the mare, and forced her back. It seemed as if he sank into her magnetically, and could thrust her back against herself.

"The fool!" cried Ursula loudly. "Why doesn't he ride away till it's gone by?"

Gudrun was looking at him with black-dilated, spellbound eyes. But he sat glistening and obstinate, forcing the wheeling mare, which spun and swerved like a wind, and yet could not get out of the grasp of his will, nor escape from the mad clamour of terror that resounded through her, as the trucks thumped slowly, heavily, horrifying, one after the other, one pursuing the other, over the rails of the crossing.

This passage comes from D. H. Lawrence's *Women in Love*, first published in 1921. The two Brangwen sisters, Ursula and Gudrun, are walking in mining country in the Midlands, and are held up at a level crossing by a colliery train. Gerald Crich, a young local landowner, is admired by Gudrun but rather despised, at this stage, by her sister.

It is difficult to show the characteristic mode of thought of such a writer in so short an example, and quite impossible to show what is happening in terms of character and personality without ranging far into what comes before and after. But something of his style and quality can be seen even within such restrictions.

One first notices, perhaps, an intense awareness of the *physical*: of the senses, sound and sight in particular; and then, more subtly, of those movements and sensations of the body itself which are called 'kinaesthetic.' One or two examples will serve, but the whole passage is full of such intense and vivid awareness of the body. "Pleased with the delicate quivering of the creature between his knees" and "sitting soft and close" tell us something important about Gerald Crich, his imperious sense of power, as well as describing the high-bred nervousness of the mare. "The sharp blasts of the chuffing engine broke with more and more force on her . . . she recoiled like a spring let go," makes the sound of the engine like a physical force, which is the way it would affect a nervous mare. "The mare rebounded like a drop of water from hot iron" is what is sometimes known as a 'synaesthetic' image: the tactile sense, in this case an acute sensation of recoil, is used to describe vividly what is in fact merely a sound. This image is also highly relevant in that the engine *is* in a sense "hot iron"; the mare in comparison is fluid in movement, sweating and with flanks like watered silk, and as antagonistic to the engine as water to a hot surface. The passage is full of such physical awareness, and this is characteristic of Lawrence; it gives nearly all his writing a personal and idiosyncratic flavour which has been widely imitated but generally without much success.

Though the total effect seems effortless and easy, the rhythms and length of sentences will often be found to be varied in a way that contributes greatly to this total effect. The second paragraph opens with short sentences: "The locomotive chuffed slowly between the banks, hidden. The mare did not like it. She began to wince away, as if hurt by the unknown noise. But Gerald pulled her back and held her head to the gate. The sharp blasts of the chuffing engine broke with more and more force on her." The effect is one of rising menace, a series of jerks, like the crashing sounds themselves. The last sentence in the passage quoted has an opposite purpose and gives the remorseless continuity of the noise, of Gerald's battle of will with the mare, and of Gudrun's terror. "As the trucks thumped slowly, heavily, horrifying, one after the other, one pursuing the other" gives this inescapable repetitiveness finely, and the apparently pointless repetition is seen to be purposeful and to play its part in the feeling of conviction derived from the passage. Lawrence can be seen continually using similar devices of repetition in his prose and also in his poetry, sometimes with an incantatory effect.

Behind this sort of detailed observation one can see even in this limited passage that some larger patterns are established, and that the inter-relations are used not merely to provide local colour or as contributions to a narrative, but have symbolic force—though it would be necessary to read the whole novel to illustrate this fully. Gerald represents the small landed aristocracy, to some degree dependent on and yet arrogantly superior to the ugly clanking train. His horse is an anachronism in a sense, but it symbolizes the aristocratic, pre-industrial ruling classes. The horse is organic, elegant, highly bred, and the train is in comparison clumsy, mechanical, dead; yet it is the train that, for the moment, dominates, and obliges Gerald to fight back. The mare is terrified but Gerald holds her, because he holds on by an act of will to his own aristocratic position against the thundering ugly future. Gudrun is terrified but also fascinated at the sight of Gerald's implacable determination; her attitude is in strong contrast to Ursula's contemptuous common-sense, which shows that she is not involved emotionally and therefore finds him merely absurd. As Gerald struggles with the mare and imposes his will on her it is as if he is imposing it also on Gudrun. Gerald's "blue eyes, full of sharp light," his "glistening half-smiling look" and "it seemed as if he sank into her magnetically"—all these expressions suggest love as well as horsemanship, and the whole passage is a metaphor of the subjugation involved in love. Finally, Gerald is high up on his mare while the two girls are humbly low on foot as well as pushed into the hedge, and this suggests their social relations, and more important, their relative psychological positions at this point in the novel.

There is, of course, a great deal more here that deserves

comment: but enough has been said to suggest that this kind of prose approximates in some ways to what we think of as poetry and will submit itself to a similar kind of analysis. On examination one finds that there is nothing that is merely decorative, and it is no more possible to cut out sentences and paragraphs than it would be from a well-organized poem. The dramatic and the sensory are co-present; and writing of this quality is miles away from the narrative pudding or patches of stuck-on 'fine' writing which characterize so many novels, including some highly successful ones.

(II)

The number of souls in this kingdom being usually reckoned one million and a half, of these I calculate there may be about 200,000 couple whose wives are breeders; from which number I subtract 30,000 couple who are able to maintain their own children (although I apprehend there cannot be so many, under the present distresses of the kingdom); but this being granted, there will remain 170,000 breeders. I again subtract 50,000 for those women who miscarry, or whose children die by accident or disease within the year. There only remain 120,000 children of poor parents annually born. The question therefore is, how this number shall be reared and provided for? which, as I have already said, under the present situation of affairs is utterly impossible by all the methods hitherto proposed. For we can neither employ them in handicraft nor agriculture; we neither build houses (I mean in the country) nor cultivate land; they can very seldom pick up a livelihood by stealing, till they arrive at six years old, except where they are of towardly parts; although I confess they learn the rudiments much earlier; during which time they can, however, be properly looked upon only as probationers; as I have been informed by a principal gentleman in the country of Cavan, who protested to me that he never knew above one or two instances under the age of six, even in a part of the kingdom so renowned for the quickest proficiency in that art.

I am assured by our merchants, that a boy or a girl before twelve years old is no saleable commodity; and even when they come to this age they will not yield above £3, or £3, 2*s.* 6*d.* at most, on the Exchange; which cannot turn to account either to the parents or kingdom, the charge of nutriment and rags having been at least four times that value.

I shall now therefore humbly propose my own thoughts, which I hope will not be liable to the least objection.

I have been assured by a very knowing American of my acquaintance in London, that a young healthy child, well nursed, is at a year old a most delicious, nourishing, and wholesome food, whether stewed, roasted, baked or boiled; and I make no doubt that it will equally serve in a *fricassée* or a *ragout*.

I do therefore humbly offer it to public consideration that of the 120,000 children already computed, 20,000 may be reserved for breed, whereof only one-fourth part to be males; which is more than we allow to sheep, black cattle, or swine; and my reason is, that these children are seldom the fruits of marriage, a circumstance not much regarded by our savages, therefore one male will be sufficient to serve four females. That the remaining 100,000 may, at a year old, be offered in sale to the persons of quality and fortune through the kingdom; always advising the mother to let them suck plentifully in the last month, so as to render them plump and fat for a good table. A child will make two dishes at an entertainment for friends; and when the family dines alone, the fore or hind quarter will make a reasonable dish, and, seasoned with a little pepper or salt, will be very good boiled on the fourth day, especially in winter.

I have reckoned upon a medium that a child just born will weigh 12 pounds, and in a solar year, if tolerably nursed, will increase to 28 pounds.

I grant this food will be somewhat dear, and therefore very proper for landlords, who, as they have already devoured most of the parents, seem to have the best title to the children.

Infant's flesh will be in season throughout the year, but more plentifully in March, and a little before and after: for we are told by a grave author, an eminent French physician, that fish being a prolific diet, there are more children born in Roman catholic countries about nine months after Lent, than at any other season; therefore, reckoning a year after Lent, the markets will be more glutted than usual, because the number of Popish infants is at least three to one in this kingdom; and therefore it will have one other collateral advantage, by lessening the number of Papists among us.

I have already computed the charge of nursing a beggar's child (in which list I reckon all cottagers, labourers, and four-fifths of the farmers) to be about 2*s.* per annum, rags included; and I believe no gentleman would repine to give 10*s.* for the carcase of a good fat child, which, as I have said, will make four dishes of excellent nutritive meat, when he has only some particular friend or his own family to dine with him. Thus the squire will learn to be a good landlord, and grow popular among his tenants; the mother will have 8*s.* net profit, and be fit for work till she produces another child.

Those who are more thrifty (as I confess the times require) may flay the carcase; the skin of which, artificially dressed, will make admirable gloves for ladies, and summer boots for fine gentlemen.

As to our city of Dublin, shambles may be appointed for this purpose in the most convenient parts of it, and butchers, we may be assured, will not be wanting; although I rather recommend buying the children alive, and dressing them hot from the knife as we do roasting pigs.

This is an extract from a pamphlet published by Jonathan Swift in 1729. Its full title is: *A Modest Proposal for preventing the Children of poor People in Ireland from being a burden to their parents or country, and for making them beneficial to the public.* The pamphlet is quite short and should certainly be read in full: but I have tried, by making a fairly lengthy extract from it, to give something of its flavour.

Not much is needed by way of historical background to explain this passage, but a few words may be helpful here. Swift spent a great deal of his life in Ireland, and from 1713 until his death in 1745 he was Dean of St Patrick's, Dublin, a position which he regarded as equivalent to exile. His most famous work, *Gulliver's Travels*, was written during this period of discontent, and he wrote extensively in defence of the Irish people and in protest against their economic and social state. This pamphlet is one of the most famous of these savage satires.

The opening paragraph deals with the statistics of the Irish population, the immense majority of whom were peasants. The tone is objective and 'scientific,' very much the tone that a journalist might use in discussing fat stock. The language is carefully adjusted to reinforce this tone: "200,000 *couple*" and "whose wives are *breeders*" both remind us of cattle, and this is sustained throughout the pamphlet. He deducts "30,000 couple who are able to maintain their own children," that is between one-sixth and one-seventh, itself a sufficiently appalling statement; but the point is made sharper by the passage in brackets: "although I apprehend there cannot be so many, under the present distresses of the kingdom," which suggests that the figure is over-generous. Then he subtracts 50,000 for miscarriages or infant deaths by accident or disease—nearly one-third of the remaining total. He then asks "how this number shall be *reared* and *provided* for?" The meaning of these expressions will become clear later. He lists "the methods hitherto proposed" for dealing with the problem, and rejects them all. Agriculture, handicrafts, building are all stagnating. The peasantry are living in derelict cottages or huts, and the implication of the bracketed phrase ("I mean in the country") is that buildings are going up only in the towns, where the richer people and the English live. He moves on directly to stealing—the only other way of getting a living; and with a completely straight face he points out that they cannot be expected to get a living thus before the age of six, "except where they are of towardly parts," that is, precocious or advanced for their age. The little anecdote about the gentleman from Cavan reinforces this judicious, almost chatty note: if even in Cavan they are not proficient thieves below six they are unlikely to be so elsewhere. The paragraph finishes with an air of having disposed of all "methods" and the ground is left clear for his own.

The next paragraph ("I am assured by our merchants . . .) makes reference to the virtual serfdom that existed in Ireland at that time, girls being sold into domestic service and boys to work on farms, ostensibly as apprentices. He quotes the financial authorities to endorse his statement that children below the age of twelve have no market value, and even at twelve "they will not yield above £3, or £3, 2*s.* 6*d.* at most on the Exchange." The last phrase gives the impression of judiciously admitting an opponent's case, and quietly suppresses the horror one must feel at the idea of selling children at all by a bland assumption that it is normal and to be expected, and by treating it as a strictly monetary matter: this "cannot turn to account" (*i.e.*, benefit) "either to the parents or the kingdom," the charge of their upkeep and clothing being at least four times that sum. This means that Irish children cost £1 a year to raise, and this is to be compared with the ten shillings for a single meal that is mentioned later. The first year, as is also stated later, costs only about two shillings because the child is being suckled at that time. But the words chosen are "nutriment" and "rags"; the second, with its deadly implication that none of them can afford proper clothes, shows far more profoundly their poverty than any positive statement of it could.

His own proposal is "humble," which echoes the "modest" of the title; and like any pamphleteer, he hopes it will "not be liable to the least objection." The next paragraph and what follows, introduced by statements in such a silky 'reasonable' tone, must surely be one of the most appalling ever written. Why "the American" is introduced I am not sure, unless he had knowledge of cannibalism among the American Indians at that time. The child must be "healthy" and "well nursed" and it will make "delicious," "nourishing," and "wholesome" food, however cooked. He actually offers recipes, and admits that he is not sure whether it will "equally serve in a *fricassée* or a *ragout*" but has no doubt that it will do so. Then he goes on to make his "modest proposal"—that one fifth of the Irish children "be reserved for breed," only a quarter of which are to be male, "which is more than we allow to sheep, black cattle, or swine": the implication here is that he is willing to be generous about it, that no one could possibly accuse him of treating them no better than animals. The reference to children being born out of wedlock and the word "savages" may appear to attack the peasantry: but these words are ironic and are the language and attitude appropriate to the kind of person he is mocking throughout. Moreover the conditions of squalor, overcrowding, and filth in which the peasants lived (as Swift knew only too well) will inevitably produce savagery. Here he says that the logical conclusion is to admit that they are cattle, and the word "serve"—used solely for animals—makes this clear. The remaining 100,000 are to be sold as food, fattened up as cattle and pigs are, and sold "to persons of quality and fortune throughout the kingdom"—they are the only people who would be able to afford them. The last sentence ("A child will make two dishes . . . especially in winter") sustains the tone of a cookery book; the terrifying grisliness of the idea of serving a whole child at an *entertainment* for friends when the circumstances call for luxury, or of a *family* dining alone on a fore or hind quarter, with its suggestion of a reasonable economy, is all the more powerful because of this calm, unflustered, business-like tone. The suppression of any suggestion or hint that anyone might object to the plan on moral, religious, or humane grounds makes a devastating effect.

Swift then deals with the weight of the child and allows himself one little bit of direct satire when he admits that the food will be "somewhat dear" and therefore appropriate for landlords, "who, as they have already devoured most of the parents, seem to have the best title ('claim') to the children." The landlords are largely responsible for the plight of the Irish peasantry; and as they have been eating them metaphorically, they may as well eat them literally. The next paragraph satirises Catholicism, but also mocks the anti-Papists, at whom the last phrase is a dig: "therefore it will have one other collateral advantage, by lessening the number of papists among us."

He then reckons the cost of rearing the child, to set it against the value of the food: he uses the term "beggar's child" descriptively, as it were, rather than rhetorically: indeed he defines "beggars" as "all cottagers, labourers, and four-fifths of the farmers"; thus ninety-five per cent of the whole Irish peasantry is quietly defined as being in a state of beggary. This is presented coolly and apparently without emotion, as a recognized fact. The child costs two shillings to rear, "rags included," and will be worth ten shillings as meat. The conclusion is equally 'logical' and calm: "thus the squire will learn to be a good landlord" (he is a bad one at present and would *improve* if he ate his tenants' children) "and grow popular among his tenants" because he is helping them to survive. "The mother will have 8*s.* net profit and be fit for work till she produces another child": here the child is to be seen by its mother solely as a source of profit, and the telling thing is that there is no suggestion that she could possibly have any feelings of love for it. Love, he implies, is a luxury which these impoverished people cannot afford.

The last two paragraphs bring home the 'realities' of the proposal in case we have still not seen the full implications and may still be able to shrug the whole thing off as an unpleasant joke. The use of the skin for "those who are more thrifty," with its 'reasonable' note in brackets ("as I confess the times require") shows with what remorseless persistence his tone is sustained: "artificially dressed" means 'prepared with art or skill,' and "fine gentlemen" implies a whole background of idle luxurious landlords living on the misery of the peasant population. The final paragraph shows an apparent wish to tidy up the details. Where shall we have our slaughterhouses? ("shambles" are butcheries or slaughterhouses). There will be plenty of butchers available, wanting to do the work; but on the whole, Swift adds calmly, the children should be bought alive and dressed "hot from the knife"—that is, prepared and cooked soon after being slaughtered. The cruel monosyllables "hot" and "knife" make their effect, and the final horrifying suggestion is that the babies should be killed in the kitchen.

This tone is sustained for three times the length of this extract. I repeat that the whole pamphlet should be read, preferably aloud, to get the complete achievement in perspective: but I cannot forebear quoting the conclusion:

> I desire those politicians who dislike my overture, and may perhaps be so bold as to attempt an answer, that they will first ask the parents of these mortals, whether they would not at this day think it a great happiness to have been sold for food at a year old in the manner I prescribe, and thereby have avoided such a perpetual scene of misfortunes as they have since gone through by the oppression of landlords, the impossibility of paying rent without money or trade, the want of common sustenance, with neither house nor clothes to cover them from the inclemencies of the weather, and the most inevitable prospect of entailing the like or greater miseries upon their breed for ever.
>
> I profess, in the sincerity of my heart, that I have not the least personal interest in endeavouring to promote this necessary work; having no other motive than the public good of my country, by advancing our trade, providing for infants, relieving the poor, and giving some pleasure to the rich. I have no children by which I can propose to get a single penny; the youngest being nine years old, and my wife past child-bearing.

This last paragraph, with its reference to "providing for infants" and its careful disclaimer of personal monetary motives, can speak for itself.

It should now be clear that Swift's main power here is in sustaining irony—an irony of unparalleled intensity. Behind the quiet tone, the lucid analysis, the calm reasonableness of the whole of the passage quoted, a savage and despairing anger is at work. Seldom has such hatred been concealed by so commonplace and familiar a tone of voice. The passage illustrates the statement that anger and bad-temper, far from being synonymous, are almost opposites: Swift is furiously angry but shows no hint of bad-temper. The coolness, even coldness of the style, may at first sight suggest a chilly and calculating temperament, but this would be a false conclusion: his heart is full of pity and warmth as well as hatred for oppression and cruelty, and only with this mask can he allow himself to speak at all. So close-knit is the texture of his irony, so unbroken the tone of the practical reasonable man, that it was possible for a foreign author of the time to have taken the *Proposal* at face value, and "to have quoted it as an instance of the extremity under which Ireland laboured." Irony consists of the mock adoption of one's opponents' views or tone, and the point here is that the proposals he makes, and the meticulous detail with which he describes them, are rendered more and not less hideous by the tone. Though we shall not, like the foreign author, take his proposals seriously, the total effect is intensely serious, indeed tragic, because it implies in every line (and irony works always by implication) that the lot of the Irish is such that even these monstrous ideas are somehow in keeping. One reads with the eye and the mind, with a sense of shock, loathing and a sort of terrified nervous laughter: but, throughout, the writer's purpose is being implacably hammered home. The strain on the mind is very great, and the destruction of any complacency complete. English, and Irish, readers of this pamphlet on its first publication must have had their consciences at least radically disturbed, and the impact has not lessened with the passage of time. In a sense history has caught up with these horrors, and lampshades and gloves of human skin were actually made in German concentration camps in the last war.

Aesthetic judgments may almost seem out of place in such a context, but we have to remember that this is a great piece of *writing*, and its power to make the mind shudder lies in the control of vocabulary, structure, and style that overlies the desperate situation he is revealing. It is radically didactic writing in one sense, but it ranges wider than the mere correction, however important, of any contemporary cruelty, indifference, or complacency, into a purging terror and pity about the human situation itself. I know of nothing more powerful in the whole of English prose.

(III)

"Now, what I want is, Facts. Teach these boys and girls nothing but Facts. Facts alone are wanted in life. Plant nothing else, and root out everything else. You can only form the minds of reasoning animals upon Facts: nothing else will ever be of any service to them. This is the principle on which I bring up my own children, and this is the principle on which I bring up these children. Stick to Facts, sir!"

The scene was a plain, bare, monotonous vault of a schoolroom, and the speaker's square forefinger emphasized his observations by underscoring every sentence with a line on the schoolmaster's sleeve. The emphasis was helped by the speaker's square wall of forehead, which had his eyebrows for its base, while his eyes found commodious cellarage in two dark caves, overshadowed by the wall. The emphasis was helped by the speaker's mouth, which was wide, thin, and hard-set. The emphasis was helped by the speaker's voice, which was inflexible, dry, and dictatorial. The emphasis was helped by the speaker's hair, which bristled on the skirts of his bald head, a plantation of firs to keep the wind from its shining surface, all covered with knobs, like the crust of a plum pie, as if the head had scarcely warehouse-room for the hard facts stored inside. The speaker's obstinate carriage, square coat, square legs, square shoulders,—nay, his very neckcloth, trained to take him by the throat with an unaccommodating grasp, like a stubborn fact, as it was,—all helped the emphasis.

"In this life, we want nothing but Facts, sir; nothing but Facts!"

The speaker, and the schoolmaster, and the third grown person present, all backed a little, and swept with their eyes the inclined plane of little vessels then and there arranged in order, ready to have imperial gallons of facts poured into them until they were full to the brim.

This is the celebrated opening of Charles Dickens's *Hard Times.* It requires no explanation beyond what it offers itself. This short passage is printed as a complete chapter entitled "The One Thing Needful," and Dickens is obviously using it as an important opening theme which is to characterize the whole of the novel, rather like the opening theme in a symphony. The speaker is a school inspector, and the other two adults mentioned are subsequently introduced as Mr Gradgrind, the owner of the school, and Mr M'Choakumchild, the schoolmaster.

The passage opens with great directness in a few sentences of dialogue. The monosyllable "Facts," with its capital letter, rapped out at intervals, usually at the end of sentences, the string of imperative verbs at the beginning and the end, the cold abstractions like "reasoning animals," "service," "principle," all contribute to the effect of a bleak utilitarianism which is really the subject of the whole novel.

The second paragraph gives the setting and describes the speaker. The "plain, bare, monotonous vault of a schoolroom," which itself emphasizes the strict utilitarianism of the room, is a sparse mean description of a sparse mean room, not worth any more words than this. It is echoed and re-emphasized by the description of the speaker. The paragraph shows some of the elaboration and proliferation which is typical of Dickens' descriptive writing; often, indeed, the elaboration is comic in effect, but here it is grimly in earnest. "The *square* forefinger *emphasized* his observations by *underscoring* every sentence"—the italicized words give the keynote, and what follows is four sentences beginning "The emphasis was helped by . . ." each acting as a hammer blow, so that the total effect is one of stifling narrowness and constriction, choking out vitality, variety, life itself. When we look at the description of the speaker more closely, we find that each detail contributes to this effect. The first sentence uses imagery that belongs to building or mensuration (the word 'architecture' would suggest something altogether too beautiful and non-utilitarian to be appropriate): "The speaker's square wall of a forehead," his eyes "commodious cellarages," "two dark caves," "overshadowed by the wall." The face is like a factory or a warehouse. The eyes, where one would hope to see some sign of life, are concealed in the hollows, and the implication is that any liveliness he might have shown has been obliterated by his brain. "The speaker's mouth was wide, thin, and hard-set": it echoes the straight lines of the eyebrows, its thinness betokens meanness, and "hard-set" suggests ruthlessness if not cruelty. His voice is "inflexible, dry, and dictatorial": these three adjectives are the very opposite of anything organic or alive, every variation, even in the rise and fall of the voice, being excluded. His hair, what hair he had, "bristled"—another kind of emphasis—"like a plantation of firs," which suggests a bleak mountain landscape. The firs, so-called 'evergreen,' have a peculiar lifelessness of colour and texture, and none of the variations one finds in deciduous trees. They protect the bald cranium, which is knobby "like the crust of a plum-pie." Here, we might think, is the charming redundancy for which Dickens is sometimes praised, but even this grotesque image is made use of: "as if the head had scarcely warehouse-room for the hard facts stored inside." The knobs are the product of too much fact-accumulation, and the "warehouse"—a beautifully chosen word—is stuffed full of hard facts which push up the surface of the skull. The last sentence in the long paragraph sums up: "obstinate carriage, square coat, square legs, square shoulders"—all of these echo the mathematical squareness of his eyebrows and mouth. His neckcloth—a nineteenth-century cravat is meant—is tight and appears almost to choke him: he is the kind of person who could not possibly wear comfortable clothes; the points of his collar hold his head rigid and become another stubborn fact. In this last sentence the structure is reversed so that the whole paragraph finishes on the key-word "emphasis." In summary, one can say that except for the 'bumps of learning' on his bald head, which symbolize his *raison d'être*, everything about him is square and straight and dry, like the "bare monotonous vault of a schoolroom," like the creed he is preaching, like the Facts themselves.

The remorseless repetitions in this descriptive passage are now capped with a repetition by the speaker: "In this life we want nothing but Facts, sir; nothing but Facts." The reader is by now reeling under the blows, and feels like the school-children who are listening to this harangue. The last paragraph gives a movement which expresses our feelings: the three adults "all backed a little." But the children are completely immobile: "the inclined plane" is a mathematical way of expressing their serried rows; they are numerically placed[1] "then and there arranged in order"; they seem as inanimate, as lacking in individuality, as uniform, as "little vessels," like a series of bottles in a factory, and they are "ready to have imperial gallons of facts poured into them," like a row of empty bottles waiting to be filled. And indeed, this philosophy of life and this view of education would regard them as such: the metaphor used is

[1] In the next chapter this idea is made even more forceful—and more appalling—when Mr Gradgrind refers to one of the children as "girl number twenty.'

exactly appropriate to the kind of 'education' which is being demonstrated.

Dickens is well known for his writing about schools, and most readers will have come across the descriptions of dreadful schools like Salem House School (in *David Copperfield*) and the more famous Dotheboys Hall and its headmaster, Wackford Squeers (in *Nicholas Nickleby*). It is widely known that his novels did a good deal towards reforming the educational system of the country and exposing its worst abuses. But here the target is a more subtle one: not the existence of cruel and sadistic schoolmasters, filthy and appalling surroundings, bad food and grossly incompetent teaching of the earlier novels, but the 'new' type of school which claimed to replace the old chaotic system with one which would be uniform, businesslike, modern—'practical,' to use a word which is typical and symptomatic. Manchester utilitarianism is the target here: this doctrine was very highly thought of and widely praised as a counter to old-fashioned methods and principles, and is an important symbol of a period that put its trust in the acquisition of wealth, the production of goods, the training of artisans to mind the new machines—and inevitably, the worship of Facts. One can hope that this sort of attitude is no longer common in schools, or in life itself: but there are unquestionably remnants still, and the joyless airlessness and rigidity that inhabits this passage is surely not unknown in our schools even now. The issue here is in fact by no means dead, and therefore the writing still has a cutting edge for us. It forces us to reconsider how much of education ought to be concerned with the accumulation of facts, and what other objectives education should have.

The method here is one of bitter satire. It is not in some ways typical of this writer; but the great warmth, sympathy, and pity which are characteristic of Dickens and among his most valuable and endearing qualities, exist here, as it were, by negation. These few lines show the sort of mentality, and, specifically, the attitude to children, that Dickens detested; and they imply richly the organic variety and pulse of life he would wish to see in place of the stifling, rigid, authoritarian fact-worship which he so vividly evokes.

(IV)

(a)

The grainy sand had gone from under his feet. His boots trod again a damp crackling mast, razorshells, squeaking pebbles, that on the unnumbered pebbles beats, wood sieved by the shipworm, lost Armada. Unwholesome sandflats waited to suck his treading soles, breathing upward sewage breath. He coasted them, walking warily. A porterbottle stood up, stogged to its waist, in the cakey sand dough. A sentinel: isle of dreadful thirst. Broken hoops on the shore; at the land a maze of dark cunning nets; farther away chalk-scrawled backdoors and on the higher beach a dryingline with two crucified shirts. Ringsend: wigwams of brown steersmen and master mariners. Human shells.

(b)

He turned from the tray, lifted the kettle off the hob and set it sideways on the fire. It sat there, dull and squat, its spout stuck out. Cup of tea soon. Good. Mouth dry. The cat walked stiffly round a leg of the table with tail on high.

—Mkgnao!

—O, there you are, Mr Bloom said, turning from the fire. The cat mewed in answer and stalked again stiffly round a leg of the table, mewing. Just how she stalks over my writing-table. Prr. Scratch my head. Prr.

Mr Bloom watched curiously, kindly, the lithe black form. Clean to see: the gloss of her sleek hide, the white button under the butt of her tail, the green flashing eyes. He bent down to her, his hands on his knees.

—Milk for the pussens, he said.

—Mrkgnao! the cat cried.

They call him stupid. They understand what we say better than we understand them. She understands all she wants to. Vindictive too. Wonder what I look like to her. Height of a tower? No, she can jump me.

—Afraid of the chickens she is, he said mockingly. Afraid of the chookchooks. I never saw such a stupid pussens as the pussens.

Cruel. Her nature. Curious mice never squeal. Seem to like it.

She blinked up out of her avid shameclosing eyes, mewing plaintively and long, showing him her milkwhite teeth. He watched the dark eyeslits narrowing with greed till her eyes were green stones. Then he went to the dresser, took the jug Hanlon's milkman had just filled for him, poured warm-bubbled milk on a saucer and set it slowly on the floor.

—Gurrhr! she cried, running to lap.

He watched the bristles shining wirily in the weak light as she tipped three times and licked lightly. Wonder is it true if you clip them they can't mouse after. Why? They shine in the dark, perhaps, the tips. Or kind of feelers in the dark, perhaps.

He listened to her licking lap. Ham and eggs, no. No good eggs with this drouth. Want pure fresh water. Thursday: not a good day either for a mutton kidney at Buckley's. Fried with butter, a shake of pepper. Better a pork kidney at Dlugacz's. While the kettle is boiling. She lapped slower, then licking the saucer clean. Why are their tongues so rough? To lap better, all porous holes. Nothing she can eat? He glanced round him. No.

These two passages come from James Joyce's *Ulysses*. The first is part of a description of Stephen Dedalus walking on the beach at Sandymount, near Dublin, the second from the chapter introducing the character of Leopold Bloom. I propose first to consider the two passages separately, and then to make a comparison between them.

Passage (*a*) looks like at first glance like a piece of direct description, but it is not long before we discover elements in it which are not merely descriptive: "that on th'unnumbered pebbles beats," "lost Armada," "isle of dreadful thirst." These are reflections of Stephen's, and they reveal that the details of the shore are not seen directly by the author, or, as it were, by a god, but that they are seen through the eyes, felt through the soles of the feet, smelt through the nostrils, transformed through the imagination, of the character experiencing them. If this passage were compared with a parallel piece of descriptive material in, say, a novel of Scott, the distinction would be immediately apparent. The latter gives a bird's eye view, an author's comments, a careful 'build-up' of atmosphere, locale, sight and sound and smell—and then puts the figure of the character in this created landscape; but here the scene exists only in terms of Stephen's experience.

He is walking from Sandymouth northwards along the shore of Dublin Bay: Ringsend is a place-name, and lies on the north, by the mouth of the River Liffey. He is presumably moving from an area of sand below the high-tide line and is now walking across the débris that is cast up by the full tide. The sensory detail is very rich here. "Grainy sand" is not merely visual but is felt through the feet, as is "the damp crackling mast." "Mast" is literally the fruit of beech and oaks found under the trees, and so, by analogy, any accumulation of débris. "Crackling" gives its surface dryness and brittleness, but it is still damp underneath where the sun has not reached it. "Razorshells" are those long bluish shells, straight-edged, curved within and razorsharp as well as looking rather like the case of an old-fashioned razor. "Squeaking pebbles" gives the sound as one walks over damp stones and they slip and grind together, and this reminds Stephen of the lines from Shakespeare's *King Lear*:

> the murmuring surge
> That on th'unnumber'd idle pebbles chafes....

Stephen gets the quotation slightly wrong ("beats" for "chafes" and the omission of "idle"). Joyce himself would never do so by accident, as he has an almost neurotic passion for minute accuracy. But Stephen remembers the essential "unnumbered" with its onomatopoeic effect: the pebbles are too numerous to count, and the word itself echoes their chafing protests as the sea rumbles over them and makes them round. "Wood *sieved* by the shipworm" describes the fragments of ships' timbers holed, generally very neatly, by marine worms, sometimes so extensively that they look honeycombed. The word "sieved" is very exact in its context, and its exactitude belongs to Stephen. "Lost Armada" is Stephen's reflection on this—the countless hulks of wrecked ships, some from the Spanish Armada itself, part of which was wrecked in the Irish Sea or nearby. The sandflat is a sort of quicksand, and the water in it is presumably stagnant. "He *coasted* them" is appropriate here because of the general feeling of coastal scenery. "Porter" is a kind of dark beer; "stogged," which may be a coined word, suggests 'stodgy,' 'lodged,' and 'soggy,' and seems exactly right for the bottle sticking out of the "cakey sand dough," which in turn suggests an uncooked cake mixture, with a peculiar kind of stickiness and a colour similar to that of the sand. The bottle is a sentinel in the surrounding flatness and evokes in Stephen's mind the "isle of dreadful thirst"—perhaps a reference to survivors of a shipwreck cast up on a waterless island in the tropics: perhaps, more remotely, the idea of a message in a bottle thrown into the sea by such people. It may also echo the title of Thomson's poem, *The City of Dreadful Night.* The idea of cast-off rubbish is continued by the "broken hoops," which may be the hoops of barrels or curved fragments of broken lobster-pots; and the eye travels up to the higher shore above the water-line, where fishing-nets are drying—"a maze of dark cunning nets" where "maze" gives their complexity. "Cunning" evokes richly the elaborate way in which they are interlaced and tied and the dexterity involved in their manufacture, the fineness of the twine of which they are made, the way in which they are folded so that the complexity of their patterning is increased, and their cunning purpose as they sweep through the water and catch fish by the gills, invisibly. From the squalid remnants on the beach through the elegant nets Stephen's eye moves to the squalid waterside with children's scribbles on the backdoors and the washing hanging on the line. "Crucified" shirts gives splendidly the position of the shirt with its two arms stretched out by the pegs. Ringsend is presumably a place where sailors retire in sight of the sea, living in small houses which suggest to Stephen the American-Indian wigwam, perhaps because the steersmen are brown with long exposure to the sea. They are "human shells" in the sense that after retirement they no longer exist except as a shell which previously contained a body—and "shells" also is appropriate to the marine imagery throughout: the old sailors are living on or near the shore, as it were cast up by the tide, like shells, but they are emptied of all the vitality and life they showed at sea, and can now only sit and stare at the element that has been their life.

The second passage describes Leopold Bloom as he gets up in the morning and prepares to take tea up to his sleeping wife. The detail throughout is familiar, domestic, commonplace. Again this is an admixture of Bloom's thoughts and reflections with the narrative. It should not be necessary to point all of these out if the method described above has been understood. but one or two general points may be made. Bloom thinks in a kind of interior dialogue: "Cup of tea soon. Good. Mouth dry"; "Wonder what I look like to her. Height of a tower? No, she can jump me"; "Wonder is it true if you clip them they can't mouse after. Why? They shine in the dark, perhaps, the tips. Or kind of feelers in the dark, perhaps." These three examples—and there are many others—show that Bloom has a perpetual awareness of the real and the physical; he is perpetually asking questions of himself, and his imagination, if it exists at all, is elementary. These three qualities are essential to an understanding of Bloom; even in this short passage his cast of mind is revealed. He is amiable and kind, as is shown by his attitude to the cat; he lives entirely on a level of immediate responses of the senses; he is relatively uneducated, though he has a mass of half-digested information, but he makes up for this by his perpetual curiosity, which could be called scientific, that is, concerned with the phenomena of the real world and its causes. He has what might be called a *Tit-Bits* type of mind. He is much concerned with his own sensations and has a sensual attitude to them: "fried with butter, a shake of pepper," "No good eggs with this drouth." He is cautious in temperament: "Nothing she can eat? He glanced round him. No." His reflections are all commonplace and everyday.

The style of the passage reflects these characteristics exactly, and the very ordinariness of the occasion—Bloom padding around the kitchen waiting to make tea—seems appropriate to his character. This does not preclude some brilliant touches of observation, though, but they too are all sensory. The four noises the cat makes are all different and on a sort of rising scale, and it is amusing to try to reproduce them with the voice. "The kettle sat there, dull and squat, its spout stuck out" gives cleverly with its heavy monosyllables the feeling of inertia as you wait for some sight or movement that suggests that it will soon boil. The cat's "avid shameclosing eyes" is one of a number of fine brush-strokes of description. "Warm-bubbled milk" is visual and tactile at once. But wherever we are given a thought of Bloom's the rhythms are jerky and flat, reflecting the essentially commonplace, kindly, curious mind behind them.

It should now be possible to compare the two passages briefly. The first is, in comparison with the second, intensely imaginative. As Stephen walks along the shore his thoughts come as casually as those of Bloom, but for Stephen the world of phenomena is material for the imagination to work on. Compare "sieved by the shipworm," "isle of dreadful thirst," "crucified shirts" with anything in the second passage and the point will be clear. Joyce is revealing his characters here, but not by traditional means. Fielding, for example, describes his characters directly from an Olympian point of view—that of a god who can see into their hearts and minds as well as knowing them as we know real people; Dickens shows his characters in action and makes us draw conclusions about their personalities; but Joyce shows us the mode, the actual *texture*, of his characters' thoughts. He puts them into typical settings in these two passages: Stephen is abstracted, solitary, reflective, Bloom domesticated, enclosed, absorbed in routine; but it is what they think about and how they see the world that distinguishes them, and each passage enables us to get right inside the being of the person concerned. The rhythms, too, reinforce these impressions. Though the thoughts of both characters are rendered in short and often fragmentary sentences, Stephen's are subtle, complex, sometimes elegant, sometimes forceful, often beautiful: in comparison Leopold's rhythms are flaccid and journalistic: indeed, he is a part-time journalist.

With the further implications of these generalizations we are not concerned, though it is perhaps worth saying that throughout this vast novel Leopold Bloom and Stephen Dedalus represent two poles of human experience: flesh and spirit, the scientific and the imaginative, prose and poetry, the man in the street and the intellectual, the here-and-now and the remote and disembodied. Dedalus is much more like Joyce himself, who once wished to be a poet: but Bloom (oddly enough from one point of view) is the hero.

This mode of writing has been labelled 'the stream of consciousness' or 'the interior monologue'; and this immensely influential book has been widely imitated. It is possible to say that it is all *too* contrived, too cerebral, too calculated, too worked-over, too much, perhaps, like a picture made of minute pieces of coloured paper stuck on with great precision and *finesse*. Certainly it contrasts strongly in style and mode of thought with Lawrence's prose discussed earlier, and you may reasonably prefer the vitality, sensitivity and organic sense of life there to the more calculated effect of these passages. But it is equally undeniable that this is a *tour de force* in its own right, and shows an extraordinary intellectual grasp and subtlety.

(V)

"But wasn't Akbar's new religion very fine? It was to embrace the whole of India."

"Miss Quested, fine but foolish. You keep your religion, I mine. That is best. Nothing embraces the whole of India, nothing, nothing, and that was Akbar's mistake."

"Oh, do you feel that, Dr Aziz?" she said thoughtfully. "I hope you're not right. There will have to be something universal in this country—I don't say religion, for I'm not religious, but something, or how else are barriers to be broken down?"

She was only recommending the universal brotherhood he sometimes dreamed of, but as soon as it was put into prose it became untrue.

"Take my own case," she continued—it was indeed her own case that had animated her. "I don't know whether you happen to have heard, but I'm going to marry Mr Heaslop."

"On which my heartiest congratulations."

"Mrs Moore, may I put our difficulty to Dr Aziz—I mean our Anglo-Indian one?"

"It is your difficulty, not mine, my dear."

"Ah; that's true. Well, by marrying Mr Heaslop, I shall become what is known as an Anglo-Indian."

He held up his hand in protest. "Impossible. Take back such a terrible remark."

"But I shall; it's inevitable. I can't avoid the label. What I do hope to avoid is the mentality. Women like—" She stopped, not quite liking to mention names; she would boldly have said "Mrs Turton and Mrs Callendar" a fortnight ago. "Some women are so—well, ungenerous and snobby about Indians, and I should feel too ashamed for words if I turned like them, but—and here's my difficulty—there's nothing special about me, nothing specially good or strong, which will help me to resist my environment and avoid becoming like them. I've most lamentable defects. That's why I want Akbar's 'universal religion' or the equivalent to keep me decent and sensible. Do you see what I mean?"

Her remarks pleased him, but his mind shut up tight because she had alluded to her marriage. He was not going to be mixed up in that side of things. "You are certain to be happy with any relative of Mrs Moore's," he said with a formal bow.

"Oh, my happiness—that's quite another problem. I want to consult you about this Anglo-Indian difficulty. Can you give me any advice?"

"You are absolutely unlike the others, I assure you. You will never be rude to my people."

"I am told we all get rude after a year."

"Then you are told a lie," he flashed, for she had spoken the truth and it touched him on the raw; it was itself an insult in these particular circumstances. He recovered himself at once and laughed, but her error broke up their conversation —their civilization it had almost been—which scattered like the petals of a desert flower, and left them in the middle of the hills. "Come along," he said, holding out a hand to each. They got up a little reluctantly, and addressed themselves to sightseeing.

This extract comes from E. M. Forster's novel *A Passage to India*, which was first published in 1924. This book is, among other things, a study of Indian reactions to British rule and the conflicts of temperament and tradition involved when India was part of the British Empire, and the British rulers lived side by side with the subject peoples of India. Aziz is a young Moslem intellectual, a doctor, who has invited a group of English guests to see the famous Marabar caves. Among them are Miss Quested, who is on her first visit to India, and Mrs Moore, whose son by her first marriage, Ronnie Heaslop, is City Magistrate for the town of Chandrapore. Adela Quested is an awkward, angular, very serious, and intensely conscientious young woman; Mrs Moore is a withdrawn and mysterious figure, often irritable but capable of a real sympathy and understanding for India which Adela can only envy and wish to achieve. Dr Aziz is an able and sensitive young man, but embodies all the difficulties and edginess inevitable when rulers and subject peoples try to live together.

The passage, which is mainly dialogue, has been chosen to show how Forster treats this immensely complex and delicate question, and how his characters emerge from dialogue and comment. The little party is sitting in the vicinity of the caves. Aziz has provided a lavish breakfast: he is delighted with his guests and is feeling expansive. Akbar was a great Mogul emperor who tried to unite India and evolved a new religion. The opening remark is from Miss Quested, who is cross-questioning Aziz, and approves of what she knows of Akbar because of his attempt to unite the whole country. Aziz, however, knows the real situation and replies that "Nothing embraces the whole of India": as a Moslem he would feel that about the Hindus and about the incoherent vastness of India, whereas Miss Quested reflects her Britishness in her wish for uniformity, and her idealism in her wish for universal brotherhood. But the real situation, as she is soon to discover, is much more difficult and 'gritty' than that. Her reply shows that she is inclined to impose her ideas on the situation: "There will *have* to be something universal in this country" is a statement of her will rather than a historical or sociological imperative. Aziz has frequently dreamed of universal brotherwood but dislikes the doctrinaire way in which Miss Quested puts it, and it is his reflection that "as soon as it was put into prose it became untrue."

" 'Take my own case,' she continued—it was indeed her own case that had animated her." The ironic, rather waspish author's comment is typical of Forster: Miss Quested discusses large abstractions with sincerity, but is really moved by small and personal immediacies. The comment is made with a reserve and coolness reminiscent of Jane Austen. She announces her forthcoming marriage, and Aziz offers formal congratulations, into which he tries to put some personal warmth ("heartiest"): but he doesn't really like Heaslop, who is rapidly deteriorating because of his official position, into a standardized representative of the ruling white caste. Fearing that she may cause his mother unease, by any oblique criticism of her fiancé, she asks permission to discuss her problem, but old Mrs Moore is evasive and passes the problem back to Miss Quested, refusing to allow herself to be involved ("It is your difficulty, not mine, my dear"). Miss Quested accepts this—she is extremely honest—and puts her problem bluntly: "By marrying Mr Heaslop, I shall become what is known as an Anglo-Indian."

This expression needs a little explanation. From one point of view the term merely means English people resident in India[1]—and therefore probably in the government service; but it carries in this dialogue, and particularly for Aziz, the meaning of an Anglo-Indian attitude—one of assuming the innate superiority of white rulers to their coloured underlings, of despising and distrusting the Indians, of refusing any real social contacts, of implacably opposing any serious Indian aspirations towards independence—in fact, a whole *ethos* which belongs to the social position. If Adela Quested marries an English official, how can she withstand the pressure to become 'one of them'—

[1] *Anglo-Indian.* This term is *now* used to describe a person of mixed English and Indian descent.

to adopt this inevitable attitude and behaviour-pattern? We are here at the core of the passage, and also of the book. Is it possible for an Englishman or woman in an India ruled by an English minority to sustain real personal relations—friendship, love—with members of a subject people? Aziz is appalled at the prospect of Miss Quested's deterioration: she is, after all, his guest, and he is trying to show in real life that social relations between the two races *are* possible. His position is in a way invidious: the lady seems insistent, and her bluntness, though admirably honest, is somehow in bad taste. Yet he knows it to be true, that she won't in fact be able to avoid becoming like the others.

The rest of the passage is a working-out of this theme. Miss Quested will be labelled by her social position and rôle, and she is honest and far-seeing enough to anticipate becoming "ungenerous and snobby about Indians." She pulls up after "Women like—" "not quite liking to mention names." Mrs Turton and Mrs Callendar, wives of the Collector and the Civil Surgeon (Aziz's superior) are typically snobbish, unimaginative 'ruling-caste' wives. When Miss Quested first came to India she was appalled by them; but already after a fortnight she feels that it would be wrong to expose them, by name, to the criticism of an Indian: the British sense of solidarity is already insidiously working on her. This is a brilliant touch and shows how the situation of ruler and ruled brings its own inevitable prejudices: she hopes to "avoid the mentality," but she has already got a little of it. She goes on to express her uncertainties about being able to sustain her present generous attitude and returns to the topic of Akbar to explain herself. This, too, cuts both ways, because Akbar failed and Miss Quested seems to be admitting that she will too.

Aziz approves of her remarks but can't bear to think of

her marriage, which will mean that she is lost for ever to any prospect of racial co-operation. He admires Mrs Moore who has shown real kindness and sympathy towards him, and tries to turn the subject; he can't praise Heaslop but he feels that any son of Mrs Moore's must have something to commend him, however hard it may be to see. But her personal happiness is not the point at issue and she insists on returning to the major point. Aziz can only say "You are absolutely unlike the others. . . . You will never be rude to my people." Miss Quested says with her usual bluntness and honesty "I am told we all get rude after a year," and this he cannot deal with because he knows it to be true: he has seen it so often. He longs to retain these free natural relations with white friends, and she is spoiling everything by forcing him to acknowledge the truth. "It was itself an insult in these particular circumstances." She is reminding him that his party is doomed in the long run to total failure, and in the process of insulting the English in India ("We all get rude after a year") she is insulting her host and the whole social nexus with which they are experimenting at the moment. He tries to 'cover up' with a laugh, but their intimacy is broken: the racial and political issues have intruded, the feeling of equality and ease has gone. Forster calls this momentary ease "civilization" and suggests its fragility and short-lived beauty in the image "like the petals of a desert flower." They are now alone in the hills. Aziz senses this and returns to the rôle of host conducting his guests on a sightseeing tour. His guests also sense the break, and get up "a little reluctantly" to see the caves.

It is very tempting to go on and show what comes next: the cave visit is in fact disastrous and becomes a *cause célèbre* which destroys the delicate balance of relationships between English and Indians in Chandrapore. These disasters obviously cast an ironic light back on the passage we have been examining, and make it appear a little oasis of civilization in the desert of racial hatred. But even on its own it illustrates many of the characteristic strengths of Forster. The character-drawing is incisive and yet subtle. There is something blundering in Adela's forthright pursuit of the truth: she is not entirely aware that frankness about the common attitudes among the English may destroy this particular occasion, when the host is an Indian and the guests both English and women—a more or less unprecedented occasion. It is a little like lovers analysing the nature and limitations of love during a love scene; and her honesty, a reflex of her angular personality, sometimes expresses itself as a loss of tact. Yet she would feel that tact would be inappropriate here and would show that the battle had been lost. Aziz is somewhat ill-at-ease throughout: his English, though excellent, is not quite English. The rhythms and constructions are faintly and subtly 'off-key': "Miss Quested, fine but foolish"; "On which my heartiest congratulations"; "my people"; "Then you are told a lie." His patches of formality, his attempts at slang, his efforts to be really intimate and relaxed, are all a little strained; and he doesn't quite know how to behave because the situation itself, though it ought to be common and familiar, is in fact very unusual. No English person, and particularly no English woman, who had been in India for a year would have accepted such an invitation from an Indian host; and indeed Aziz probably couldn't have made it. So the dialogue, which might at first sight seem a mere patch of theorizing about race relations, emerges as a sample of the inherent difficulties as well.

This kind of dialogue illustrates personality in action, and shows on a small scale the range of such an inter-racial relationship—cross-currents, misunderstandings, dishonesties as well as more direct self-revelation. The author's comments show a rich imagination ("as soon as it was put into prose it was untrue"; "her error broke up their conversation—their civilization it had almost been—which scattered like the petals of a desert flower") and an acid irony ("she would boldly have said 'Mrs Turton and Mrs Callendar' a fortnight ago"; " 'Then you are told a lie,' he flashed, for she had spoken the truth and it touched him on the raw.") This is writing of exceptional urbanity and poise, with exceptional grasp and imaginative power; it shows an unwillingness to oversimplify or dramatize the issues it deals with, and gives something of the very texture of human relations in all their complexity and subtlety.

(VI)

A general silence succeeded. Each was thoughtful. Fanny made the first interruption by saying, "I wonder that I should be tired with only walking in this sweet wood; but the next time we come to a seat, if it is not disagreeable to you, I should be glad to sit down for a little while."

"My dear Fanny," cried Edmund, immediately drawing her arm within his, "how thoughtless I have been! I hope you are not very tired. Perhaps," turning to Miss Crawford, "my other companion may do me the honour of taking an arm."

"Thank you, but I am not at all tired." She took it, however, as she spoke, and the gratification of having her do so, of feeling such a connexion for the first time, made him a little forgetful of Fanny. "You scarcely touch me," said he. "You do not make me of any use. What a difference in the weight of a woman's arm from that of a man! At Oxford I have been a good deal used to have a man lean on me for the length of a street, and you are only a fly in the comparison."

"I am really not tired, which I almost wonder at; for we must have walked at least a mile in this wood. Do not you think we have?"

"Not half a mile," was his sturdy answer; for he was not yet so much in love as to measure distance, or reckon time, with feminine lawlessness.

"Oh, you do not consider how much we have wound about. We have taken such a very serpentine course; and the wood itself must be half a mile long in a straight line, for we have never seen the end of it yet, since we left the first great path."

"But if you remember, before we left that first great path, we saw directly to the end of it. We looked down the whole vista, and saw it closed by iron gates, and it could not have been more than a furlong in length."

"Oh, I know nothing of your furlongs, but I am sure it is a very long wood; and that we have been winding in and out ever since we came into it; and therefore when I say that we have walked a mile in it, I must speak within compass."

"We have been exactly a quarter of an hour here," said Edmund, taking out his watch. "Do you think we are walking four miles an hour?"

"Oh, do not attack me with your watch. A watch is always too fast or too slow. I cannot be dictated to by a watch."

A few steps farther brought them out at the bottom of the very walk they had been talking of; and standing back, well shaded and sheltered, and looking over a ha-ha into the park, was a comfortable-sized bench, on which they all sat down.

"I am afraid you are very tired, Fanny," said Edmund, observing her; "why would not you speak sooner? This will be a bad day's amusement for you, if you are to be knocked up. Every sort of exercise fatigues her so soon, Miss Crawford, except riding."

"How abominable in you, then, to let me engross her horse as I did all last week! I'm ashamed of you and of myself, but it shall never happen again."

"*Your* attentiveness and consideration make me more

sensible of my own neglect. Fanny's interest seems in safer hands with you than with me."

"That she should be tired now, however, gives me no surprise; for there is nothing in the course of one's duties so fatiguing as what we have been doing this morning—seeing a great house, dawdling from one room to another—straining one's eyes and one's attention—hearing what one does not understand—admiring what one does not care for. It is generally allowed to be the greatest bore in the world, and Miss Price has found it so, though she did not know it."

"I shall soon be rested," said Fanny: "to sit in the shade on a fine day, and look upon verdure, is the most perfect refreshment."

Earlier in this book I have quoted a definition of a novel as "the kind of thing Jane Austen writes." Certainly the art of the novel seems at its purest and most complete in her work, particularly in the three late novels *Mansfield Park*, *Emma*, and *Persuasion*. But though there seems no doubt that Jane Austen represents a peak, if not the peak, in the novel's development so far, there are initial difficulties. The chief of these is that her *milieu* is so totally foreign to most modern readers, and at first sight so restricted and limited. She writes in entirely contemporary (early nineteenth-century) terms of the daily life of what might now be called the upper-middle classes, generally in rural settings against a background of country houses; a scoffer might describe the chief contents of the novels as tittle-tattle over the tea-cups among women with too little to do and too much to say. Male students particularly may find something stifling in the atmosphere of a Jane Austen novel when it is first looked at. But these limitations are apparent rather than real: Jane Austen knows this particular section of society with such consummate thoroughness and sees it with such depth and such involvement, side by side with ironic detachment, that her restricted canvas turns out to be a source of strength rather than weakness. She seems to illustrate the assertions that a great artist can use any raw material, that scope and range are not essential, and that what really matters is depth. So great is her intellectual grasp, so deep are her powers of understanding, that it is not absurd to say that some of her best work has a Shakespearean richness and depth.

This passage comes from *Mansfield Park*, and the texture of this novel is so closely-knit that I have found it very difficult to choose a passage; here "everything links up with everything else" to such an extent that nothing shorter than a chapter can illustrate her full powers, and one feels a wish to quote all that leads up to the chosen passage and all that follows. So I would strongly suggest that the whole incident (Chapters Eight, Nine, and Ten) of the novel should be read; the passage quoted will then fall into place, just as a particular theme which cannot be fully 'realized' out of its context falls into place in a symphony. Perhaps a better metaphor would be from the game of chess: we are looking at the twenty-ninth move and need to know the first twenty-eight and the next forty to see the full significance of this one move.

Indeed this section of the novel is rather like a game of chess, with the people moving through the grounds of Sotherton Park in directions and distances determined by their characters and appetites, but in unpredictable order and interaction. Edmund Bertram with his two sisters is paying a visit to Sotherton, the country seat of a Mr Rushworth, who is engaged to marry the elder. Accompanying them on this visit are Henry Crawford and his sister Miss Crawford, and Fanny Price, a ward of the Bertrams. Fanny has been accepted on sufferance by most of the Bertram family, but Edmund has been kind to her and she in turn becomes devoted to him. Edmund is attracted, however, to Miss Crawford, who is lively and vivacious and rather scatter-brained. The party has been conducted round the house on a long tour of inspection and has retired to the garden for fresh air and rest, and to get away from the prosy meanderings of Mrs Rushworth. Miss Crawford, who is flirting with Edmund, has been talking sarcastically about the Church, and has then found to her embarrassment, that Edmund is intending to take orders. After an uneasy conversation in which Edmund has gently but firmly rebuked her for her levity on the subject, the passage opens. Edmund has the devoted Fanny on one side and the flirtatious Miss Crawford on the other: he is half-ashamed of his liking for the latter.

A general silence succeeded. Each was thoughtful.

Edmund is reflecting on Miss Crawford's limitations; Fanny cannot help being concerned with the obvious devotion he shows to Miss Crawford, who in turn is reconsidering Edmund now that he has told her of his career; she is a snob, and she has said that "a clergyman is nothing," but Edmund is the only person present with whom she can flirt. Fanny has found the whole situation exhausting and wishes to sit down. Edmund, realizing that she has been neglected during his long duel with Miss Crawford, immediately invites her to take his arm and sees the opportunity of inviting Miss Crawford to do the same. This makes the support he offers to Fanny turn into an excuse to make physical contact with Miss Crawford. She claims that she is "not at all tired," pointing up a contrast between her vitality and Fanny's weakness, but nevertheless takes his arm, thereby showing to Fanny that it is done out of affection and not need. Thrilled by this contact, he forgets that it is Fanny who is tired, and begs Miss Crawford to lean more on him: the quiet omission of any such appeal to Fanny shows that he is indifferent to her touch and not concerned with her feelings. "You are only a fly in the comparison," compliments Miss Crawford on her lightness and delicacy, and yet asks her to show a little more ardour. For some time from now on Edmund allows Miss Crawford to monopolize the conversation, and we picture Fanny being dragged along and treated with as much feeling as a sack of potatoes. Miss Crawford repeats that she is not tired, to rub in the meaningfulness of her taking arms, and she shows coquetry in both offering (taking his arm) and withdrawing (refusing to lean on him at all). Though not tired, she feels as if she has walked a mile, and she is quite indifferent to her surroundings. This side of her character is defined a little earlier:

> she had none of Fanny's delicacy of taste, of mind, of feeling; she saw nature, inanimate nature, with little observation; her attention was all for men and women, her talents for the light and lively.

The sensation of having walked a long way may be a shaft directed at Fanny's presence, and certainly reflects her general impulsiveness and impatience. Edmund's reply to her remark about having walked a mile is accompanied by one of Jane's Austen' delicious 'asides': "he was not yet so much in love as to measure distance, or reckon time, with feminine lawlessness." The comment gives him a certain sturdy commonsense and makes clear that though fascinated, he is not yet besotted. Moreover, he wants to prolong the walk and the physical contact that accompanies it. Miss Crawford argues for the sake of argument, indulging in a quick scatter-brained chatter that reveals her lively personality but gives no indication of any conscious process of thinking. Her two parallel replies "Oh, I know nothing of your furlongs" and "Oh, do not attack me with your watch" show that when sticking to her point she can ignore anything so trifling as a fact; this gives her a certain charming *insouciance*, to Edmund at least, but makes her conversation exhausting, at any rate to poor Fanny, who herself is desperately sincere, diffident in conversation, and retiring in personality, all of which admirable qualities put her at a disadvantage in this situation. There is also a feeling that Miss Crawford is offering herself as a sample of femininity, and her conversation is so illogical that she is letting down the whole sex by indulging in it, especially as Edmund is sometimes censorious about female chatter. That he offers no criticism here can only exacerbate the situation for Fanny; his usual critical powers are in abeyance, and to wish him to use them would be pushful on Fanny's part, if not a proof of jealousy.

They come to a seat (a "ha-ha" is a sunken fence or wall), and Edmund speaks to Fanny. It is the act of sitting down which draws his attention to her again. "Observing her" can mean "looking at her" but also carries the meaning 'noticing (again) that she is there,' 'becoming aware of her.' He then discusses her health with Miss Crawford. This seems to shows solicitude for Fanny, but Fanny will feel as though she is being pinned out on a board for inspection, like an entomological specimen. Some contrast is implied between her fatigue and Miss Crawford's admirable vitality. Edmund, in fact, is being clumsy, and using Fanny's health merely as a topic for further talk with Miss Crawford, and perhaps to cover his embarrassment at not bringing her before into the conversation. The references to riding go back to the previous week when Edmund has been helping

Miss Crawford to ride and thereby preventing Fanny from using the horse; before Miss Crawford arrived, he had devoted a lot of time to teaching Fanny, so this is a sore subject for her. "Sensible" means 'aware': it took Miss Crawford's insight to draw attention to his neglect. Miss Crawford's apology may be meant well, but carries a note of patronage; and Edmund exaggerates its merits and turns it into a compliment to her. She has rebuked him for neglecting Fanny, but is aware that the more "abominable" the neglect the more intense his attraction towards Miss Crawford must have been. His comment that "Fanny's interest seems in safer hands with you than with me" is tactless in that it is uncomfortably true from Fanny's point of view and therefore makes her neglect more painful (it is even acknowledged), and credits Miss Crawford with a generosity and selflessness of which she is quite incapable, as Fanny already knows. Miss Crawford's last speech "That she should be tired now . . ." shows her superficiality: "hearing what one does not understand—admiring what one does not care for." This superficiality, however, is credited not to her but to Fanny: Miss Crawford, who is in fact speaking for herself in her usual style, insists that this general incomprehensibility and boringness is what has made Fanny tired, and makes it worse for Fanny by concluding that "Miss Price has found it so, though she did not know it." The last clause makes Fanny stupidly unaware of her own reactions as well as generally unresponsive and easily bored. The 'cattiness' is not the main note, but it is present; and Fanny does not even attempt to answer it directly. She limits herself to implicit thanks and shows that she wishes to be thought completely happy and at ease: "to sit in the shade on a fine day, and look upon verdure, is the most perfect refreshment." Not much later, however, Edmund finds an excuse for going off with the restless

Miss Crawford, and it is she who gives him the opportunity of being alone with her by saying "I must move, resting fatigues me"—this, within a minute or two of Fanny's sitting down and stressing her fatigue. Fanny says that she is rested too, but Edmund

> urged her remaining with an earnestness which she could not resist, and she was left on the bench to think with pleasure of her cousin's care, but with great regret that she was not stronger.

Her great "regret" is that she is not strong enough to stand up to Miss Crawford.

Jane Austen's art is of that kind which conceals art. The movement is effortless, the dialogue apparently trifling and genteel; nothing to speak of seems to happen. Yet to look closely at any part of her novels is to become aware that the restrictions are not constricting; that though there is little or no excitement in them, there is the keenest delight in nuances of conduct and emotion. No sentence is wasted: none of the dialogue or description is mere narrative or mere local colour, and everything contributes to a richer understanding of her characters. These novels are splendid to read aloud, and seem to benefit from the leisurely pace that reading aloud involves. The general inference a study of her work suggests is that a writer doesn't need huge canvases or crowd scenes, vast atmospheric descriptions or violence, to produce intensity: the intelligence and sensitivity of the writing is so great that it convinces us very quickly of the reality of even so remote a society as hers. The intensity and *éclat* which in a modern novel might be produced by some shattering event can within this world be produced by a phrase or a glance or a touch on the arm. Jane Austen, unlike Dickens, knew her range exactly and never moved outside it; the result is that in the best novels everything rings true and everything contributes. The quiet simple tone conceals this rich complexity, and the closer the reading the more depth is revealed. To show so much of human life within the confines of the village and county gentry is a rare and subtle art; Fielding, with all his warmth and talent, is a coarse windbag in comparison. In this sense the novel may be said to have begun with Jane Austen, and it seems likely that her art has not yet been surpassed.

Part Three

WORK FOR THE STUDENT

THE next three chapters are arranged to correspond with those in Part Two, and consist of poems, passages from drama, and passages of prose for examination by the student. Each passage is followed by a series of questions intended to act as a guide to what to look for; if they are worked through, orally or in written form, a good deal that is important in the passages should be revealed. Again there has been no attempt to be comprehensive, though again it is hoped that a fair range of material will be found.

The poetry section contains an anonymous religious poem, a song lyric, two love poems, a humorous poem, and a passage from Chaucer. The dramatic passages are mostly from Shakespeare, but include also two passages from modern plays. Of the prose passages, three come from novels, two from essays, and one from a historical work.

Chapter Seven

SOME POEMS FOR CLOSE READING

(I)

A Lyke-Wake Dirge

This ae nighte, this ae nighte,
    —Every nighte and alle,
Fire and fleet and candle-light,
    And Christe receive thy saule.

When thou from hence away art past,
    —Every nighte and alle,
To Whinny-muir thou com'st at last;
    And Christe receive thy saule.

If ever thou gavest hosen and shoon,
    —Every nighte and alle,
Sit thee down and put them on;
    And Christe receive thy saule.

If hosen and shoon thou ne'er gav'st nane
    —Every nighte and alle,
The whinnes sall prick thee to the bare bane;
    And Christe receive thy saule.

From Whinny-muir when thou mayst pass,
    —Every nighte and alle,
To Brig o' Dread thou com'st at last;
    And Christe receive thy saule.

From Brig o' Dread when thou may'st pass,
—Every nighte and alle,
To Purgatory fire thou com'st at last,
And Christe receive thy saule.

If ever thou gav'st meat or drink,
—Every nighte and alle,
The fire shall never make thee shrink;
And Christe receive thy saule.

If meat or drink thou ne'er gav'st nane,
—Every nighte and alle,
The fire will burn thee to the bare bane;
And Christe receive thy saule.

This ae nighte, this ae nighte,
—Every nighte and alle,
Fire and fleet and candle-lighte,
And Christe receive thy saule.

1. This anonymous ballad has a burden or chorus-line throughout. Suggest from your knowledge of ballads what function this repetition has (*a*) for the original ballad audience, (*b*) for a modern reader.

2. The poem gives a narrative of a journey. Point out the verses which describe this journey. "Whinnes" are gorse-bushes, and "brig" means bridge; with this information describe the journey in your own words, and say what is meant by "from hence," "Whinny-muir," "Brig o' Dread," (*a*) literally and then (*b*) in terms of the sustained metaphor of the whole poem.

3. What is the connexion between verses 3 and 4? Show how they relate to the previous verse (2) and the following one (verse 5). Then trace the similar connection between verses 7 and 8, and show what relationship they have with verse 6.

4. What is the connexion between "this ae nighte" and the

burdenline "Every nighte and alle"? "Fire and fleet and candle-light" probably means 'embers, water and house-room.' What rôle is played by the first and last verses?

5. Attempt a general evaluation of the poem, trying to show from what source it draws its strength, what assumptions are made about the beliefs of the audience, what effect is made by its economy of language and the repeated chorus, especially the last line of each verse. This dirge was one of those sung at a "wake," or family gathering, held while the corpse ("lyke") was awaiting burial. A "dirge," as the word is used nowadays, suggests something mournful, if not morbid. Try to decide whether the total effect of this poem is morbid or 'bracing.'

(*Note.* There is a setting of this poem by Benjamin Britten for tenor voice, horn, and strings in a work called *Serenade*. If this can be played in class—at least twice, because its effect is not immediately made—an interesting discussion of the setting might take place after the work has been done on the poem.)

(II)

O Mistress mine, where are you roaming?
O, stay and hear—your true love's coming,
  That can sing both high and low:
Trip no further, pretty sweeting;
Journeys end in lovers' meeting,
  Every wise man's son doth know.

What is love? 'tis not hereafter;
Present mirth hath present laughter;
  What's to come is still unsure:
In delay there lies no plenty:
Then come kiss me, sweet and twenty!
  Youth's a stuff will not endure.

WILLIAM SHAKESPEARE

1. This poem is a song, and is sung by the clown in *Twelfth Night*. What features of the poem make it suitable for singing? In particular, what elements of rhythm and climax have the two verses in common? If you set the first verse to music, would your setting suit the second verse without modification?

2. Suggest a meaning for "pretty sweeting," "'tis not hereafter," "In delay there lies no plenty."

3. Remembering that in Shakespeare's time girls were married very young in comparison with modern practice, suggest another reading of "sweet and twenty" as well as the usual one (beautiful and twenty years old).

4. What is the force of "roaming" and "trip"? How do they relate to "journey's end"?

5. The general tone of the song is warm and positive. Where do you detect a note of sadness? Does this detract from the warmth and ardour of the rest? If not, why not?

(*Note.* An interesting addition to the study of this poem can be made if some of the many settings can be heard—either with a gramophone, or piano and voice. Seventeenth-century versions can be compared with nineteenth-century or modern ones. The test should be not only in the intrinsic musical merits of the setting, but in the success with which the whole of the poem as a poem is rendered in musical terms.)

(III)

Ther was also a Nonne, a PRIORESSE,
That of hir smyling was ful simple and coy;
Hir gretteste ooth was but by seynte Loy;
And she was cleped madame Eglentyne.
Ful wel she song the service divyne,
Entuned in hir nose ful semely;
And Frensh she spak ful faire and fetisly,
After the scole of Stratford atte Bowe,
For Frensh of Paris was to her unknowe.

At mete wel y-taught was she with-alle;
She leet no morsel from hir lippes falle,
Ne wette hir fingres in hir sauce depe.
Wel coude she carie a morsel, and wel kepe,
That no drope ne fille up-on hir brest.
In curteisye was set ful muchel hir lest.
Hir over-lippe wyped she so clene,
That in hir coppe was no ferthing sene
Of grece, whan she dronken hadde hir draughte.
Ful semely after hir mete she raughte,
And sikerly she was of greet desport,
And ful plesaunt, and amiable of port,
And peyned hir to countrefete chere
Of court, and been estatlich of manere,
And to ben holden digne of reverence.
But, for to speken of hir conscience,
She was so charitable and so pitous,
She wolde wepe, if that she sawe a mous
Caught in a trappe, if it were deed or bledde.
Of smale houndes had she, that she fedde
With rosted flesh, or milk and wastel-breed.
But sore wept she if oon of hem were deed,
Or if men smoot it with a yerde smerte:
And al was conscience and tendre herte.
Ful semely hir wimpel pinched was;
Hir nose tretys; hir eyen greye as glas;
Hir mouth ful smal, and ther-to softe and reed;
But sikerley she hadde a fair forheed;
It was almost a spanne brood, I trowe;
For, hardily, she was nat undergrowe.
Ful fetis was hir cloke, as I was war.
Of smal coral aboute hir arm she bar
A peire of bedes, gauded al with grene;
And ther-on heng a broche of gold ful shene,
On which ther was first write a crowned A,
And after, *Amor vincit omnia.*

GEOFFREY CHAUCER

Note. This passage comes from the Prologue to Chaucer's *Canterbury Tales.* This introduction gives character sketches of thirty or so people who are travelling on horseback as pilgrims to the shrine of Thomas à Becket at Canterbury Cathedral. They give a sharp picture of people who seem at first typical representatives of various trades and professions, but who reveal themselves also as intensely individual. These descriptions are brilliant vignettes of personality, and they cast a great deal of light on the period; but above all they are poetry in their own right. The language is what is known as Middle English (Chaucer died in 1400), and naturally presents certain difficulties to the modern reader: but these difficulties are not so extensive as may be imagined, and it is surprising how much of this is intelligible with careful reading. Nevertheless some words are no longer used, some have changed their meanings, and there are fairly extensive changes in pronunciation. The major one which concerns us here is that the final 'e' is frequently pronounced: a little practice in reading the verse aloud (though to do it properly needs a good deal of training) will show us how this final 'e' is frequently needed to make up the ten syllables. For example; in the following lines, the italicized '*e*' is pronounced rather like the last syllable in 'further':

> Hir over lipp*e* wyped she so clene
> That in hir copp*e* was no ferthing sene
> Of grec*e*, when she dronken hadde hir draughte.

This point is raised later in the questions.

1. What are the first things that strike the poet about the Prioress (lines 1 to 4)? What indications of character do these lines offer?

2. How did she sing in church? "Fetisly" means 'excellently.' The lines about her French are a standard joke, and often quoted by those who know nothing else of Chaucer: but in view of the date, can you suggest what else could be meant except a sneer at her bad French?

3. Paraphrase what is said about the Prioress's table manners.

What does "mete" mean here? "Lest" means 'delight': translate the line in which this word appears. What do these lines add to our picture of the Prioress? What light do they cast on the manners of the day?

4. 'She reached daintily after her food, and indeed she was lively and sportive.' Of which lines is this a rough translation? 'She took great pains to imitate courtly manners, to be stately in her demeanour.' What is there in these lines that suggest that Chaucer is gently mocking his subject? Which words mean 'to be considered worthy of'?

5. Having read the passage introduced by "But, for to speken of hir conscience," suggest modern English equivalents of "conscience," "charitable," "pitous." Paraphrase the two examples given of "conscience" ("yerde" is a stick and "smerte" means 'sharply').

6. A "wimpel" (modern English 'wimple') is a covering for the neck. What was hers like? "Tretys" means long and well-shaped; "hardily" means the same as "sikerly." Describe her appearance in modern English. Which of the lines describing her beauty would be thought odd in modern times?

7. Her clothing is briefly described ("fetis" means well-made). Why is she wearing beads? (The "gaudies" were the large beads). "*Amor vincit omnia*" means 'love conquers all.' "*Amor*" may mean charity here: if it does, how is it appropriate to the Prioress's personality? Is there any element of irony present? In what way is it an effective ending?

8. Take the following lines and underline the *e*'s that should be pronounced:

(*a*) Of smale houndes had she, that she fedde
With rosted flesh, or milk and wastel-breed.

(*b*) Entuned in hir nose ful semely;

(*c*) And peyned hir to countrefete chere.

9. Where do you think that Chaucer is being ironic in this passage? Is his tone affectionate, sneering, mocking? Gentle, sarcastic, admiring?

(IV)

The Mosquito

When did you start your tricks,
Monsieur?

What do you stand on such high legs for?
Why this length of shredded shank,
You exaltation?

Is it so that you shall lift your centre of gravity upwards
And weigh no more than air as you alight upon me,
Stand upon me weightless, you phantom?

I heard a woman call you the Winged Victory
In sluggish Venice.
You turn your head towards your tail, and smile.

How can you put so much devilry
Into that translucent phantom shred
Of a frail corpus?

Queer, with your thin wings and your streaming legs,
How you sail like a heron, or a dull clot of air,
A nothingness.

Yet what an aura surrounds you;
Your evil little aura, prowling, and casting a numbness on
my mind.

That is your trick, your bit of filthy magic:
Invisibility, and the anaesthetic power
To deaden my attention in your direction.

But I know your game now, streaky sorcerer.

Queer, how you stalk and prowl the air
In circles and evasions, enveloping me,
Ghoul on wings
Winged Victory.

Settle, and stand on long thin shanks
Eyeing me sideways, and cunningly conscious that I am
 aware,
You speck.

I hate the way you lurch off sideways into air
Having read my thoughts against you.

Come then, let us play at unawares,
And see who wins in this sly game of bluff.
Man or mosquito.

You don't know that I exist, and I don't know that you
 exist.
Now then!

It is your trump,
It is your hateful little trump,
You pointed fiend,
Which shakes my sudden blood to hatred of you:
It is your small, high, hateful bugle in my ear.

Why do you do it?
Surely it is bad policy.

They say you can't help it.

If that is so, then I believe a little in Providence protecting
 the innocent.
But it sounds so amazingly like a slogan,
A yell of triumph as you snatch my scalp.

Blood, red blood
Super-magical
Forbidden liquor.

I behold you stand
For a second enspasmed in oblivion.
Obscenely ecstasied
Sucking live blood,
My blood.

Such silence, such suspended transport,
Such gorging,
Such obscenity of trespass.

You stagger
As well as you may.
Only your accursed hairy frailty,
Your own imponderable weightlessness
Saves you, wafts you away on the very draught my anger makes in its snatching.

Away with a paean of derision,
You winged blood-drop.

Can I not overtake you?
Are you one too many for me,
Winged Victory?
Am I not mosquito enough to out-mosquito you?

Queer, what a big stain my sucked blood makes
Beside the infinitesimal faint smear of you!
Queer, what a dim dark smudge you have disappeared into!

D. H. LAWRENCE

1. This poem comes from a collection called *Birds, Beasts, and Flowers* which D. H. Lawrence wrote mostly in Italy (this latter point is worth remembering, for Tuscany is a malarial area, where the mosquitos are common). What on a first reading strikes you as odd about the poem? How does it differ from most of the poetry you have previously read (*a*) in terms of form (*b*) in content and attitude?

2. What do you think the poet gains from using free verse here? Is such free verse really 'chopped-up prose'? What elements in the language, structure, rhythms of this poem seem to you to *belong* to poetry? Give some examples.

3. Early in the poem two aspects of the mosquito seem to be stressed—its physical minuteness and the way it suggests evil. Point out expressions in the first seven 'verses' that describe each of these aspects.

4. There are a number of questions in the first quarter of the poem. What purpose have these questions, since the mosquito obviously can't answer?

5. Comment on and explain the following expressions: "Monsieur," "shredded shank," "translucent," "frail corpus," "aura." At what point in the poem does the mosquito first fly?

6. What is the "Winged Victory"? (Look it up if necessary.) Why did the woman use this name for the mosquito? Why is Venice here called "sluggish"?

7. In what respect does the mosquito "sail like a heron"? What does "a dull clot of air" mean? What word in the next verse contradicts "a nothingness"? Express in your own words what the mosquito's "bit of filthy magic" is. What, in particular, does "anaesthetic" mean here? Why is the single sentence "But I know your game now, streaky sorcerer" given a 'verse' on its own?

8. Explain "enveloping" in the next verse. Why is "Winged Victory" repeated here? What is the tone of "you speck"? How does it compare with "you exaltation"? When does the mosquito seem aware of the human being? Isn't this contradicted by "You don't know that I exist"?

9. Where does Lawrence show confidence in his power to

defeat the mosquito? Where is this confidence shaken? What is "your hateful little trump"? Paraphrase the poet's reflections about this "trump".

10. What is the point of the lines beginning "Blood, red blood"? What is the mosquito doing at this point? What is the poet doing? What is meant by "You stagger/As well as you may"? What physical gesture does the poet make in this verse? Why does he fail?

11. Why is the mosquito now a "winged blood-drop"? Explain "Am I not mosquito enough to out-mosquito you?" What has happened in the last verse?

12. Do you think writing of this kind is in danger of being diffuse and 'sprawling'? Do you feel the lack of a regular rhythm or of rhymes? What advantages do you think this fluidity and freedom give the poet for this particular subject?

13. Would you say that Lawrence gives here the essence of the mosquito? Is his tone affectionate, disgusted, horrified, ruefully amused, bewildered? Write a short general evaluation of the poem.

(V)

Lollocks

By sloth on sorrow fathered,
These dusty-featured Lollocks
Have their nativity in all disordered
Backs of cupboard drawers.

They play hide and seek
Among collars and novels
And empty medicine bottles,
And letters from abroad
That never will be answered.

Every sultry night
They plague little children,
Gurgling from the cistern,
Humming from the air,
Skewing up the bed-clothes,
Twitching the blind.

When the imbecile agèd
Are over-long in dying
And the nurse drowses,
Lollocks come skipping
Up the tattered stairs
And are nasty together
In the bed's shadow.

The signs of their presence
Are boils on the neck,
Dreams of vexation suddenly recalled
In the middle of the morning,
Languor after food.

Men cannot see them,
Men cannot hear them,
Do not believe in them—
But suffer the more,
Both in neck and belly.

Women can see them—
O those naughty wives
Who sit by the fireside
Munching bread and honey,
Watching them in mischief
From corners of their eyes,
Slily allowing them to lick
Honey-sticky fingers.

Sovereign against Lollocks,
Are hard broom and soft broom,
To well comb the hair,
To well brush the shoe,
And to pay every debt
As it falls due.

ROBERT GRAVES

Note. If you know, or can find out, what "gremlins" are in relation to aircraft, this may help you to get 'inside' the poem. You may then, after you have done the work on this poem, be able to complete the following:

gremlin: aeroplane: pilot: lack of total control:: lollocks: ?:?:?.

1. This is a light poem, in the sense that it makes no claim to profundity and its tone is amused and amusing. The central problem is, of course, in the title, which is a coined word. Kenneth Allott has called this poem a "small, perfectly acceptable example of myth-making." After reading it through silently and then reading it aloud, or hearing it read, attempt a first approximate definition of the central figure. At this stage, what do you think lollocks are?

2. What does the first line mean? Why this parentage? In particular, what does "on" mean in "by sloth on sorrow fathered"? Why are the lollocks "dusty-featured"? Say what picture this adjective gives you. Where are they born, and why?

3. What is the connexion between verse two and the previous verse? Why are the medicine bottles empty? Why will the letters never be answered?

4. What new dimension is given in verse three? Why do they come particularly on sultry nights? Do the lollocks themselves gurgle and hum? (This is a very difficult question.) What

is the difference between "gurgle" and "hum" on the one hand, and "skew up" and "twitch" on the other?

5. What is the connexion between the "imbecile agèd" and the letters, the medicine bottles, the cisterns and the bedclothes? Why is the nurse drowsy? Why should lollocks be appropriate to "the *tattered* stairs"? What picture do you get from "are nasty together"? Why "in the bed's *shadow*?"

6. Verse five moves on to a different aspect of lollocks. What have the three "signs of their presence" in common?

7. What new aspect is introduced in verse six? Why do men "suffer *the more*," and why "Both in neck and belly"? What makes this verse particularly amusing, in relation to the poet himself?

8. Why should women be able to see them? What is the attitude of the "naughty wives" to lollocks? What is the point of mentioning that they are sitting by the fireside "munching bread and honey"? Why do they see them only "from corners of their eyes"?

9. What does "sovereign" mean (compare 'a sovereign remedy')? How would the 'recipes' given keep lollocks away? What have the brooms, the comb, and the hairbrush to do with it? What help will it be to pay debts as they fall due?

10. What contribution do the rhythms of this poem make to its total effect? How do you think it should be read aloud? How will you prevent it from turning into prose when heard with the ear only? Point out some expressions which could not occur in prose. Where does it rhyme internally, or externally? Why?

11. Attempt now a comprehensive definition of lollocks according to Robert Graves. The words 'domestic' and 'neglect' may be wanted. What other circumstances can you suggest, in your own home, where lollocks might arise? Do you find this poem rather futile? If you do, say why. If not, give reasons. Is the poem charming, ingenious, original, unintelligible, piffling? Suggest other adjectives in your evaluation.

(VI)

To Marguerite (II)

Yes! in the sea of life enisled,
With echoing straits between us thrown,
Dotting the shoreless watery wild,
We mortal millions live *alone*.
The islands feel the enclasping flow.
And then their endless bounds they know.

But when the moon their hollows lights,
And they are swept by balms of spring,
And in their glens, on starry nights,
The nightingales divinely sing;
And lovely notes, from shore to shore,
Across the sounds and channels pour—

Oh! then a longing like despair
Is to their farthest caverns sent;
For surely once, they feel, we were
Parts of a single continent!
Now round us spreads the watery plain—
Oh might our marges meet again!

Who order'd, that their longing's fire
Should be, as soon as kindled, cool'd?
Who renders vain their deep desire?
A God, a God their severance ruled!
And bade betwixt their shores to be
The unplumbed, salt, estranging sea.

MATTHEW ARNOLD

1. This poem is a sustained metaphor, and the main key to its understanding is to grasp the full implications of the metaphor. What is symbolized, first, by "the sea" and "the islands"?

2. In verse one, consider the exact implications of "echoing straits," "the shoreless watery wild," "the enclasping flow," "endless bounds." Why, do you think, does the verse start with "Yes!"? Why is "*alone*" italicized?

3. In what sense do verses two and three go together? (Consider the grammar.) "Moon," "balms," "starry," "nightingales" are traditional 'romantic' words to evoke springtime and associated ideas. What *particular* rôle do they play here?

4. What geological discoveries or theories of the period are glanced at in verse three? What do you feel is meant by "caverns"? What is "they" in "they feel"?

5. There is a sharp change of tone in verse four; try to describe it. What "deep desires" are "rendered vain"? What expression is parallel to this one? What effect does the break in line two of verse four have (Should be,/as soon as kindled,/cool'd)? What sort of "God" is the poet thinking of in line four?

6. What is the effect of the accumulation of adjectives in the last line? Account for each adjective. What else is suggested by the adjectives in relation to the noun?

7. After you have done this detailed work, attempt a general evaluation of the poem. How successfully is the major metaphor managed, and are its implications also successfully embodied? Relate the theme of the poem to the 'motto' on the title-page of E. M. Forster's *Howard's End*—"Only Connect". Is the poem poignant? Despairing? Nostalgic? Resigned? Tragic? Suggest adjectives or phrases which seem to you to define its tone.

(VII)

The Sunne Rising

Busie old foole, unruly Sunne,
Why dost thou thus,
Through windowes, and through curtaines call on us?
Must to thy motions lovers seasons run?
Sawcy pedantique wretch, goe chide
Late schoole boyes, and sowre prentices,
Goe tell Court-huntsmen, that the King will ride,
Call countrey ants to harvest offices;
Love, all alike, no season knowes, nor clyme,
Nor houres, dayes, moneths, which are the rags of time.

Thy beames, so reverend, and strong
Why shouldst thou thinke?
I could eclipse and cloud them with a winke,
But that I would not lose her sight so long:
If her eyes have not blinded thine,
Looke, and to morrow late, tell mee,
Whether both the India's of spice and Myne
Be where thou leftst them, or lie here with mee.
Aske for those Kings whom thou saw'st yesterday,
And thou shalt heare, All here in one bed lay.

She is all States, and all Princes, I,
Nothing else is.
Princes doe but play us; compar'd to this,
All honor's mimique; All wealth alchimie.
Thou sunne art halfe as happy as wee,
In that the world's contracted thus;
Thine age askes ease, and since thy duties bee
To warme the world, that's done in warming us.
Shine here to us, and thou art every where;
This bed thy center is, these walls, thy spheare.

JOHN DONNE

1. This is a love poem, though it is very different from what you may associate with such a term. One quality you may find surprising or even shocking, is that it has a great deal of wit, and a strong sense of assurance, even of arrogance. Point out some instances of each in the poem.

2. Why is the poet angry with the sun at the outset? Where in the first verse does he claim (*a*) implicitly (*b*) explicitly, that lovers are not bound by any of the ordinary rules of nature?

3. Explain the following expressions:

(*a*) . . . goe chide
Late schoole boyes, and sowre prentices

(*b*) Call countrey ants to harvest offices

(*c*) . . . the rags of time

4. Explain the inversion which opens the second verse. What does the poet mean by "I could *eclipse* and *cloud* them with a winke"? Why will he not do so? Where does he pay his beloved a special compliment about the beauty of her eyes? How is the reference to the "India's of spice" (the spice islands of the East) made relevant here? Why must the sun "tell me" "*to-morrow late*"?

5. How did the sun see Kings yesterday? How does the opening of verse three link with the ending of verse two? Explain "Princes doe but play us." In what sense is "the world contracted thus"? Quote the lines which show what the poet means.

6. If the mood of the opening is one of angry contempt at being awakened, what is the mood of the ending? In what sense is this change a progress, and what has happened to the room, and the sun, during the poem?

7. Where is the sun patronized? Point out two occasions on which its age is stressed. Why? Explain these words as used in their contexts in the poem: "pedantique," "reverend,"

"mimique," "alchimie." What is appropriate about "eclipse," "cloud," "center," "spheare." in relation to the subject-matter?

8. Write a paragraph summarizing what is new to you in love poetry of this kind. T. S. Eliot has said that this kind of poetry reveals "the intellect at the tip of the senses." What do you think he means?

Chapter Eight

SOME DRAMATIC PASSAGES FOR CLOSE READING

(I)

BURGUNDY. Since, then, my office hath so far prevail'd,
That, face to face and royal eye to eye,
You have congreeted, let it not disgrace me,
If I demand, before this royal view,
What rub or what impediment there is,
Why that the naked, poor, and mangled Peace,
Dear nurse of arts, plenties, and joyful births,
Should not, in this best garden of the world,
Our fertile France, put up her lovely visage?
Alas, she hath from France too long been chased!
And all her husbandry doth lie on heaps,
Corrupting in its own fertility.
Her vine, the merry cheerer of the heart,
Unprunèd dies; her hedges even-pleach'd,
Like prisoners wildly overgrown with hair,
Put forth disorder'd twigs; her fallow leas
The darnel, hemlock, and rank fumitory,
Do root upon, while that the coulter rusts,
That should deracinate such savagery;
That even mead, that erst brought sweetly forth
The freckled cowslip, burnet, and green clover,
Wanting the scythe, all uncorrected, rank,
Conceives by idleness, and nothing teems
But hateful docks, rough thistles, kecksies, burs,
Losing both beauty and utility.
And as our vineyards, fallows, meads and hedges,
Defective in their natures, grow to wildness,

Even so our houses, and ourselves and children,
Have lost, or do not learn for want of time,
The sciences that should become our country;
But grow, like savages—as soldiers will,
That nothing do but meditate on blood—
To swearing, and stern looks, diffus'd attire,
And every thing that seems unnatural.
Which to reduce into our former favour,
You are assembled: and my speech entreats
That I may know the let, why gentle Peace
Should not expel these inconveniences,
And bless us with her former qualities.

This passage comes from Shakespeare's *Henry V*. Henry has decisively won the battle of Agincourt against the French, and the Duke of Burgundy is acting as intermediary between the English and French authorities. This is his opening speech in the presence of the English and French courts, asking what obstacles there are to a peace settlement and praying that peace shall return to France.

1. Write a rough précis of this passage, keeping the original order of the argument.

2. What expressions from the opening are parallel to those of the end? What is the purpose of this repetition?

3. Put into modern English:

> . . . all her husbandry doth lie in heaps
> Corrupting in its own fertility.

Show in detail how this is a key idea in the whole speech, and how Burgundy illustrates it.

4. In the speech there are three lines giving names of plants. What have the plants in each line in common, and what rôle do the lists of names play? Try to relate the idea behind these lines to (*a*) an Elizabethan audience (*b*) a modern audience.

5. Consider the image which compares hedges with prisoners,

and the one which compares children with soldiers. What makes them appropriate?

6. Explain, if necessary by looking up, the following words and expressions: "congreeted," "rub," "put up," "husbandry," "even-pleach'd," "coulter," "deracinate," "erst," "kecksies," "the let."

7. Burgundy speaks of the effect on human beings as well as on the landscape. What parallel does he draw?

8. What is meant in this speech by "arts" and "sciences"? Be as exact as you can.

9. What force has this speech as an argument against war?

(II)

SEXTON. Master constable, let these men be bound, and brought to Leonato's: I will go before and show him their examination. [*Exit.*

DOGBERRY. Come, let them be opinion'd.
VERGES. Let them be in the hands——
CONRADE. Off, coxcomb!
DOGBERRY. God's my life, where's the sexton? let him write down—the prince's officer, coxcomb.—Come, bind them.—Thou naughty varlet!
CONRADE. Away! you are an ass, you are an ass!
DOGBERRY. Dost thou not suspect my place? dost thou not suspect my years? O that he were here to write me down an ass!—but, masters, remember that I am an ass; though it be not written down, yet forget not that I am an ass.—No, thou villain, thou art full of piety, as shall be proved upon thee by good witness. I am a wise fellow; and, which is more, an officer; and, which is more, a householder; and, which is more, as pretty a piece of flesh as any is in Messina; and one that knows the law, go to; and a rich fellow enough, go to; and a fellow that hath had losses; and one that hath two gowns, and everything hand

some about him.—Bring him away.—O that I had been writ down an ass! [*Exeunt.*

This passage comes from Shakespeare's *Much Ado About Nothing.* Conrade and Borachio, two drunken rogues, have been arrested by the watchmen of Messina when they are discussing a plot. Dogberry is the Constable of the Watch; Verges is a headborough (his second-in-command). The Sexton is relatively educated and can write, but he leaves to report to Leonato, Governor of Messina, and is therefore not present when Conrade calls Dogberry an ass.

1. Make a list of Dogberry's verbal blunders in this passage, and say in each case what word he wanted. To what extent does the humour lie in these mistakes?

2. Consider the final speech in some detail. Try to analyse the mood of the opening, the rôle of his self-congratulation ("I am a wise fellow . . . as any is in Messina") and any change of tone in the latter half of the sentence ("and one that knows the law . . . everything handsome about him").

3. Explain the meaning of "as pretty a piece of flesh as any is in Messina," "a fellow that hath had losses," "one that hath two gowns." Make a comment on the order of terms in his description of himself.

4. Why exactly does Dogberry wish to be "written down an ass"? What does *he* mean by "masters, remember that I am an ass"? What is the dramatic effect of this declaration (*a*) on the other members of the watch, who respect and admire him, (*b*) on Conrade and Borachio (*c*) on the audience? In particular, what does he intend by his last repetition of this wish, and what effect, as a 'curtain-line,' does it have on the audience?

5. Draw a comparison between this last speech and Bottom's speech when he awakens from his enchantment in *A Midsummer Night's Dream* (Act IV, Scene I): "When my cue comes . . . I shall sing it at her death." Try to show how far the two speeches represent humour and personality of a similar kind, and how far they offer a contrast.

(III)

GHOST. But know, thou noble youth,
The serpent that did sting thy father's life
Now wears his crown.
HAMLET. O my prophetic soul!
My uncle!
GHOST. Ay, that incestuous, that adulterate beast,
With witchcraft of his wit, with traitorous gifts,—
O wicked wit and gifts, that have the power
So to seduce!—won to his shameful lust
The will of my most seeming-virtuous queen:
O, Hamlet, what a falling-off was there!
From me, whose love was of that dignity,
That it went hand in hand even with the vow
I made to her in marriage; and to decline
Upon a wretch, whose natural gifts were poor
To those of mine!
But virtue, as it never will be moved,
Though lewdness court it in a shape of heaven,
So lust, though to a radiant angel link'd,
Will sate itself in a celestial bed,
And prey on garbage.
But soft! methinks I scent the morning air;
Brief let me be.—Sleeping within my orchard,
My custom always in the afternoon,
Upon my secure hour thy uncle stole,
With juice of cursed hebenon in a vial,
And in the porches of mine ears did pour
The leperous distilment; whose effect
Holds such an enmity with blood of man,
That, swift as quicksilver, it courses through
The natural gates and alleys of the body;
And, with a sudden vigour, it doth posset
And curd, like eager droppings into milk,
The thin and wholesome blood: so did it mine;

And a most instant tetter bark'd about,
Most lazar-like, with vile and loathsome crust
All my smooth body.
Thus was I, sleeping, by a brother's hand
Of life, of crown, of queen, at once dispatch'd:
Cut off, even in the blossoms of my sin,
Unhousel'd, disappointed, unanel'd;
No reckoning made, but sent to my account
With all my imperfections on my head:
O, horrible! O, horrible! most horrible!
If thou hast nature in thee, bear it not;
Let not the royal bed of Denmark be
A couch for luxury and damn'd incest.
But, howsoever thou pursuest this act,
Taint not thy mind, nor let thy soul contrive
Against thy mother aught: leave her to heaven
And to those thorns that in her bosom lodge
To prick and sting her. Fare thee well at once!
The glow-worm shows the matin to be near,
And 'gins to pale his uneffectual fire:
Adieu, adieu, adieu! remember me.

This passage comes from Shakespeare's *Hamlet*. Denmark has lost its king Hamlet, who was reported to have been bitten by a snake while asleep in his orchard. His brother Claudius inherits the throne and marries his widow Gertrude. Hamlet, the son of the dead king, encounters his father's ghost on the battlements of the castle at Elsinore and hears from it the true story of his death.

1. Part of the Ghost's speech is narrative. Tell the story in your own words.

2. The first third or so of the speech is largely reflective. Where does this part end? Name the one aspect of Claudius' crime that is first emphasized, and paraphrase the generalization that derives from it. Where do you find a concentration of 's' sounds? What effect does this have?

3. What is the force of

> But soft! methinks I scent the morning air;
> Brief let me be?

4. What words in the narrative section of the speech suggest speed? Why are these words so used? Explain "posset," "eager," "tether." What have these words in common with one another, and also with "lazar," "droppings," "sudden"?

5. Where, particularly, does the speech seem slow in movement and where swift?

6. Explain "Cut off, even in the blossoms of my sin": another line, a little later, gives a paraphrase of it.

7. What instructions does the Ghost give to Hamlet? Quote and paraphrase the lines concerned.

8. Consider the following uses of language and explain how they are appropriate: "seeming-virtuous," "a falling-off," "to decline upon a wretch," "my secure hour," "the porches of mine ears," "the natural gates and alleys of the body." Explain the two lines about the glow-worm.

9. Where does the speech show pathos, as against righteous indignation?

10. When you have answered the other questions, but not before, attempt a paraphrase of the whole speech.

(IV)

PORTIA. Dear my lord,
Make me acquainted with your cause of grief.
BRUTUS. I am not well in health, and that is all.
PORTIA. Brutus is wise, and, were he not in health,
He would embrace the means to come by it.
BRUTUS. Why, so I do.—Good Portia, go to bed.
PORTIA. Is Brutus sick,—and is it physical
To walk unbraced, and suck up the humours
Of the dank morning? What, is Brutus sick,—
And will he steal out of his wholesome bed,

To dare the vile contagion of the night,
And tempt the rheumy and unpurgèd air
To add unto his sickness? No, my Brutus;
You have some sick offence within your mind,
Which, by the right and virtue of my place,
I ought to know of: and, upon my knees,
I charm you, by my once-commended beauty,
By all your vows of love, and that great vow
Which did incorporate and make us one,
That you unfold to me, yourself, your half,
Why you are heavy; and what men to-night
Have had resort to you,—for here have been
Some six or seven, who did hide their faces
Even from darkness.
BRUTUS. Kneel not, gentle Portia.
PORTIA. I should not need, if you were gentle Brutus.
Within the bond of marriage, tell me, Brutus,
Is it excepted I should know no secrets
That appertain to you? Am I yourself
But, as it were, in sort or limitation,—
To keep with you at meals, comfort your bed,
And talk to you sometimes? Dwell I but in the suburbs
Of your good pleasure?

This passage comes from Shakespeare's *Julius Caesar*. Brutus, a noble Roman, has been approached by some leading citizens to persuade him to join a conspiracy to murder Julius Cæsar, whom they believe about to become a dictator. Brutus has been receiving visitors secretly during the night to discuss this plot, and his wife, Portia, aware that he is deeply troubled but ignorant of the cause, is pressing him to reveal his thoughts and the source of his evident anxiety.

1. In which expressions is the third person used by Portia where we should now expect the second? What is the effect of this?

2. In what parts of the passage is the time of day stressed or

referred to? Where are contemporary (Elizabethan) views about health expressed? What significance do you attach to "suck up," "dank," "vile contagion," "rheumy and unpurgèd air"? What word means 'healthy' and how does it come to have such a meaning?

3. Point out a line of Brutus' dialogue which is entirely monosyllabic. What is the effect of this?

4. What does Portia mean by "the right and virtue of my place"? What is "that great vow"? What single word in Portia's speech emphasizes the sense of identity between married people?

5. Which lines describe the conspirators? What characteristics are emphasized in the lines?

6. What is the meaning, as used in the passage, of the following expressions: "unbraced," "wholesome," "heavy," "resort," "gentle," (in "if you were gentle Brutus"), "excepted," "sort"?

7. Explain the last metaphor in the passage. How is it particularly appropriate in a Roman play? How does it summarize Portia's speeches?

8. Portia, though only a lightly sketched character, emerges in this play as a fine person, showing firmness of mind, tenderness, loyalty, and persistence. Instance examples of these qualities in the lines quoted.

(V)

IAGO. Good heaven, the souls of all my tribe defend
From jealousy!
OTHELLO. Why, why is this?
Think'st thou I'ld make a life of jealousy,
To follow still the changes of the moon
With fresh suspicions? No; to be once in doubt
Is once to be resolved: exchange me for a goat,
When I shall turn the business of my soul

To such exsufflicate and blown surmises,
Matching thy inference. 'Tis not to make me jealous
To say my wife is fair, feeds well, loves company,
Is free of speech, sings, plays, and dances well;
Where virtue is, these are more virtuous:
Nor from mine own weak merits will I draw
The smallest fear or doubt of her revolt;
For she had eyes, and chose me. No, Iago;
I'll see before I doubt; when I doubt, prove;
And, on the proof, there is no more but this,—
Away at once with love or jealousy!

This passage comes from Shakespeare's *Othello*. Othello, a general and a Moor, has married the young Venetian Desdemona; and Iago his lieutenant, for his own purposes, has been hinting that she is unfaithful to her husband. He is clever enough, however, to warn Othello against jealousy, but Othello is already half persuaded that the accusation is just and Desdemona false.

1. This speech comes from a long and brilliant scene in which Othello is brought by Iago from a state of contentment to one of almost murderous jealousy. What can Iago gain by warning Othello against jealousy, when in fact he is trying to stimulate it?

2. Where in his speech does Othello envisage a tortured future of jealousy? What word apart from "jealousy" is repeated throughout the speech, and in what way is it important?

3. Where does Othello show any uncertainty about his worthiness for her love and on what grounds? What counter-argument does he offer to this doubt? Why are love and jealousy contradictory for him?

4. What exactly does "a life of jealousy" mean? In what sense would he "follow still the changes of the moon"? Why "the moon"?

5. Paraphrase the expression "to be once in doubt Is once to be resolv'd". Where does he contradict this later?

6. What does "exchange me for a goat" mean? Why "goat"? "Exsufflicate" means 'inflated': what other word has a parallel meaning? What unpleasant associations has this parallel word? What does "matching thy inference" mean?

7. Where in the speech does Othello try to make himself be reasonable?

8. Wilson Knight has spoken of a characteristic beauty of language in this play which he calls "the Othello music." Do you detect this music anywhere in this speech? Which lines or expressions seem to hiss or to spit? Where is this speech dignified? What emotional elements conflict with the dignity?

(VI)

INQUISITOR. You wrestle in vain with the devil for her soul, my lord: she will not be saved. Now as to this matter of the man's dress. For the last time, will you put off that impudent attire, and dress as becomes your sex?

JOAN. I will not.

D'ESTIVET (*pouncing*). The sin of disobedience, my lord.

JOAN (*distressed*). But my voices tell me I must dress as a soldier.

LADVENU. Joan, Joan: does not that prove to you that the voices are the voices of evil spirits? Can you suggest to us one good reason why an angel of God should give you such shameless advice?

JOAN. Why, yes: what can be plainer commonsense? I was a soldier living among soldiers. I am a prisoner guarded by soldiers. If I were to dress as a woman they would think of me as a woman; and then what would become of me? If I dress as a soldier they think of me as a soldier, and I can live with them as I do at home with my brothers. That is why St Catherine tells me I must not dress as a woman until she gives me leave.

COURCELLES. When will she give you leave?

JOAN. When you take me out of the hands of the English soldiers, I have told you that I should be in the hands of the Church, and not left night and day with four soldiers of the Earl of Warwick. Do you want me to live with them in petticoats?

LADVENU. My lord: what she says is, God knows, very wrong and shocking; but there is a grain of worldly sense in it such as might impose on a simple village maiden.

JOAN. If we were as simple in the village as you are in your courts and palaces, there would soon be no wheat to make bread for you.

CAUCHON. That is the thanks you get for trying to save her, Brother Martin.

This passage comes from Bernard Shaw's *St Joan*. Joan, a village girl, has seen visions which have led her to join the French army and eventually to lead it against the English. The Church fears that her teachings and influence will undermine its authority, and after she has been imprisoned by the English under the Earl of Warwick she is handed over for examination by the spiritual arm, the Bishop's court with the Inquisition participating. If the court decides that she is guilty of heresy it will hand her back to the secular arm and she will be burnt to death at the stake.

D'Estivet is the prosecutor; Cauchon the Bishop of Beauvais; de Courcelles a young canon; Ladvenu an ascetic young Dominican. Joan is chained by the ankles, and the Executioner stands behind her.

1. One of Joan's offences at which her opponents pretend horror, is her insistence on wearing men's clothes. This passage shows the attitude of the authorities, and of Joan herself, to this matter. Summarize her arguments in your own words.

2. Show where the Inquisitor moves from general and spiritual issues to a specific accusation about something manifest and, from his point of view, unarguable.

3. Can you gather anything from D'Estivet's solitary intervention of his attitude to Joan and her trial?

4. Contrast D'Estivet's attitude with that of Ladvenu. Examine Ladvenu's two speeches and show what conclusions you reach, on this evidence, about his sympathy and his

intelligence. If D'Estivet is 'rigid,' what is Ladvenu? Where does Ladvenu make a concession to what he believes to be the view of the prosecution?

5. Where is Joan tactless? Where does she show emotion? Where does she present an argument? Is it convincing? Where is the question of social class stressed, by whom, and what is the effect?

6. What is Ladvenu's Christian name? Who do you think is "my lord"?

7. Can you detect Cauchon's attitude to Joan from this passage? Make a list of those in the court who want her convicted. Who wants to save her?

8. What features suggest to you that this scene would be effective on the stage?

(VII)

SECOND KNIGHT. No one regrets the necessity for violence more than we do. Unhappily, there are times when violence is the only way in which social justice can be secured. At another time, you would condemn an Archbishop by vote of Parliament and execute him formally as a traitor, and no one would have to bear the burden of being called murderer. And at a later time still, even such temperate measures as these would become unnecessary. But, if you have now arrived at a just subordination of the pretensions of the Church to the welfare of the State, remember that it is we who took the first step. We have been instrumental in bringing about the state of affairs that you approve. We have served your interests; we merit your applause; and if there is any guilt whatever in the matter, you must share it with us.

FIRST KNIGHT. Morville has given us a great deal to think about. It seems to me that he has said almost the last word, for those who have been able to follow his very subtle reasoning. We have, however, one more speaker, who has I think another point of view to express. If there are any who are still unconvinced, I think that Richard Brito, coming as he does of a family distinguished for its loyalty to the Church, will be able to convince them. Richard Brito.

FOURTH KNIGHT. The speakers who have preceded me, to say nothing of our leader, Reginald Fitz Urse, have all spoken very much to the point. I have nothing to add along their particular lines of argument. What I have to say may be put in the form of a question: *Who killed the Archbishop?* As you have been eye-witnesses of this lamentable scene, you may feel some surprise at my putting it in this way. But consider the course of events. I am obliged, very briefly, to go over the ground traversed by the last speaker. While the late Archbishop was Chancellor, no one, under the King, did more to weld the country together, to give it the unity, the stability, order, tranquillity, and justice that it so badly needed. From the moment he showed himself to be utterly indifferent to the fate of the country, to be, in fact, a monster of egotism. This egotism grew upon him, until it became at last an undoubted mania. I have unimpeachable evidence to the effect that before he left France he clearly prophesied, in the presence of numerous witnesses, that he had not long to live, and that he would be killed in England. He used every means of provocation; from his conduct, step by step, there can be no inference except that he had determined upon a death by martyrdom. Even at the last, he could have given us reason: you have seen how he evaded our questions. And when he had deliberately exasperated us beyond human endurance, he could still have easily escaped; he could have kept himself from us long enough to allow our righteous anger to cool. That was just what he did not wish to happen; he insisted, while we were still inflamed with wrath, that the doors should be opened. Need I say more? I think, with these facts before you, you will unhesitatingly render a verdict of Suicide while of Unsound Mind. It was the only charitable verdict you can give, upon one who was, after all, a great man.

1. These speeches come at the end of T. S. Eliot's play *Murder in the Cathedral*, which was written for production at the Canterbury Festival of 1935. After their murder of Thomas à Becket, which takes place on the stage, the four knights address the audience directly to justify the murder. What do you think will be the dramatic effect of the knights' speaking directly to the audience?

2. Name three of the four knights and say which is which. Which of them is the leader? The Second Knight is earlier described as a specialist in statecraft and constitutional law. What aspects of his speech belong specifically to the twelfth century? What aspects strike you as contemporary?

3. Instance circumstances in which you think it would be true that "there are times when violence is the only way in which social justice can be secured." What is the force of "secured"? What do you think of the statement as an argument in this context? What trick of argument is played at the end of his speech?

4. How does the First Knight offer support for the Second? With what reservations? What special plea does he make for the Fourth Knight? What relevance has this in fact?

5. What is the effect of the Fourth Knight's rhetorical question "*Who killed the Archbishop?*" Comment on the use of the following words and expressions in his speech: "lamentable," "undoubted," "provocation," "righteous." Where is the statement that Becket was "a monster of egotism" contradicted? Does his prophecy make him to blame for his subsequent death? Is the "inference" quoted a sound one, and what other explanation can you offer? What do you think of the argument that Becket deliberately "exasperated us beyond human endurance"? Does it conflict with anything in the Second Knight's speech?

6. What do you think of the "verdict of Suicide while of Unsound Mind"? Which word is palpably false? How has the speaker tried to justify this word? What effect is made on the audience by the concluding sentence, in particular by "charitable" and "a great man"?

7. Try to summarize what kind of a speech the Fourth Knight makes. What is there that is suave about his manner, and what is specious about his arguments?

8. Eliot said about this play, "I wanted to bring home to the audience the contemporary relevance of the situation." What do you find in the passage quoted that is (*a*) generally relevant to modern times and problems (*b*) specifically relevant to 1935?

Chapter Nine

SOME PROSE PASSAGES FOR CLOSE READING

(I)

But I must here take leave a little longer to discontinue this narration: and if the celebrating the memory of eminent and extraordinary persons, and transmitting their great virtues, for the imitation of posterity, be one of the principal ends and duties of history, it will not be thought impertinent, in this place, to remember a loss which no time will suffer to be forgotten, and no success or good fortune could repair. In this unhappy battle was slain the lord viscount Falkland; a person of such prodigious parts of learning and knowledge, of that inimitable sweetness and delight in conversation, of so flowing and obliging a humanity and goodness to mankind, and of that primitive simplicity and integrity of life, that if there were no other brand upon this odious and accursed civil war, than that single loss, it must be most infamous, and execrable to all posterity.

Turpe mori, post te, solo non posse dolore

Before this parliament, his condition of life was so happy that it was hardly capable of improvement. Before he came to twenty years of age, he was master of a noble fortune, which descended to him by the gift of a grandfather, without passing through his father or mother, who were then both alive, and not well enough contented to find themselves passed by in the descent. His education for some years had been in Ireland, where his father was lord deputy; so that, when he returned into England, to the possession of his fortune, he was unentangled with any acquaintance or friends, which usually grow up by the custom of conversation, and therefore was to make a pure election of his company, which he chose by other rules than were prescribed to the young nobility of that time. And it cannot be denied, though he admitted some few to his friendship for the agreeableness of their natures, and their undoubted affection to him, that his familiarity and friendship, for the most part, was with men of the most eminent and sublime parts, and of untouched reputation in point of integrity; and such men had a title to his bosom.

1. This is an extract from Clarendon's *History of the Rebellion and Civil Wars in England* (1642–49) and describes the Lord Falkland who was Secretary of State in 1641 and died at the battle of Newbury in 1643, fighting against the Cromwellian forces. Point out any elements in the style which seem to you to belong to that period, or at any rate not to be modern, under three headings (*a*) words no longer used (*b*) words now used in a different sense from those of the passage (*c*) phrases or grammatical devices.

2. Paraphrase and simplify the opening sentence. What do you think of this view of the purpose of history?

3. Explain the following expressions as used in the passage: "impertinent," "will suffer to be forgotten," "prodigious parts," "unentangled," "a pure election."

4. In the second sentence ("In this unhappy battle . . .") what exactly is meant by "flowing," "brand," "execrable *to* all humanity"? In what respect is the Civil War blamed here?

5. Find out the meaning of the Latin 'tag,' and if possible, its source. What rôle does this line play in such a passage? Is it used to show Clarendon's learning? If not, why not? (Try to consider why it would be less appropriate in a piece of modern prose).

6. In what two major ways was Falkland's "condition of life" particularly happy? How did his education affect his subsequent friendships? How are friendships generally formed, according to Clarendon?

7. What do you suppose were the "rules" that "were prescribed to the young nobility of that time"? How did Falkland's

friendships differ? What two classes of friends did he adopt? Which men had "a title to his bosom" and what does this expression mean?

8. Attempt a general comment on the style of this passage. How mainly, apart from detail, does it differ from the modern prose you are familiar with? Particularly, try to comment on the sentence structure. Is the general effect dignified, pompous, long-winded, abstract? What assumptions are made about the reader?

(II)

There had not been such a winter for years. It came on in stealthy and measured glides, like the moves of a chess-player. One morning the few lonely trees and the thorns of the hedgerows appeared as if they had put off a vegetable for an animal integument. Every twig was covered with a white nap as of fur grown from the rind during the night, giving it four times its usual stoutness; the whole bush or tree forming a staring sketch in white lines on the mournful gray of the sky and horizon. Cobwebs revealed their presence on sheds and walls where none had ever been observed till brought out into visibility by the crystallizing atmosphere, hanging like loops of white worsted from salient points of the out-houses, posts and gates.

After this season of congealed dampness came a spell of dry frost, when strange birds from behind the North Pole began to arrive silently on the upland of Flintcomb-Ash; gaunt spectral creatures with tragical eyes—eyes which had witnessed scenes of cataclysmal horror in inaccessible polar regions of a magnitude such as no human being had ever conceived, in curdling temperatures that no man could endure; which had beheld the crash of icebergs and the slide of snow-hills by the shooting light of the Aurora; been half blinded by the whirl of colossal storms and terraqueous distortions; and retained the expression of feature that such scenes had engendered. These nameless birds came quite near to Tess and Marian, but of all they had seen which humanity would never see, they brought no account. The traveller's ambition to tell was not theirs, and, with dumb impassivity, they dismissed experiences which they did not value for the immediate incidents of this homely upland—the trivial movements of the two girls in disturbing the clods with their hackers so as to uncover something or other that these visitants relished as food.

Then one day a peculiar quality invaded the air of this open country. There came a moisture which was not of rain, and a cold which was not of frost. It chilled the eyeballs of the twain, made their brows ache, penetrated to their skeletons, affecting the surface of the body less than its core. They knew that it meant snow, and in the night the snow came. Tess, who continued to live at the cottage with the warm gable that cheered any lonely pedestrian who paused beside it, awoke in the night, and heard above the thatch noises which seemed to signify that the roof had turned itself into a gymnasium of all the winds. When she lit her lamp to get up in the morning she found that the snow had blown through a chink in the casement, forming a white cone of the finest powder against the inside, and had also come down the chimney, so that it lay sole-deep upon the floor, on which her shoes left tracks when she moved about. Without, the storm drove so fast as to create a snow-mist in the kitchen; but as yet it was too dark out-of-doors to see anything.

Note. This passage describes a winter at Flintcomb-Ash farm, "a starve-acre place" where Tess, the heroine of Thomas Hardy's novel, *Tess of the D'Urbervilles,* is working with Marian in the fields, lifting swedes. "Hackers" are hooked forks with which the swedes are lifted.

1. This is a very idiosyncratic passage of prose. What makes it so? Compare the opening and final paragraphs with the middle one. Which is more convincing? Why?

2. In the first paragraph, explain "integument," "worsted," "salient," Comment on these images: "like the moves of a chess-player," "a white nap as of fur grown from the rind during the night," "a staring sketch," "loops of white worsted."

3. Point out some of the learned words in the second paragraph. Do you find this paragraph over-written? What is the length and form of the characteristic sentence here?

4. What change in pace and rhythm occurs at the opening of the third paragraph? What change of subject-matter does it reflect? Describe in your own words the "peculiar quality" that invaded the air. What in this paragraph shows that Tess is probably a field labourer? What small details in this paragraph give one a sense of the weather and the place?

5. What weaknesses of prose style do you detect in this passage? What would you say, on the evidence of this passage alone, are the predominant weaknesses and strengths of this writer? Do you see anything to suggest that he might be a good lyrical poet, or a rather questionable philosophical one?

(III)

Like Mr Wilkie Collins, I, too, have been asked to lay some of my literary experiences before the readers of the *Universal Review*. It occured to me that the *Review* must be indeed universal before it could open its pages to one so obscure as myself; but, nothing daunted by the distinguished company among which I was for the first time asked to move, I resolved to do as I was told, and went to the British Museum to see what books I had written. Having refreshed my memory by a glance at the catalogue, I was about to try and diminish the large and ever-increasing circle of my non-readers when I became aware of a calamity that brought me to a standstill, and indeed bids fair, so far as I can see at present, to put an end to my literary existence altogether.

I should explain that I cannot write unless I have a sloping desk, and the reading-room of the British Museum, where alone I can compose freely, is unprovided with sloping desks. Like every other organism, if I cannot get exactly what I want I make shift with the next thing to it; true, there are no desks in the reading-room, but, as I once heard a visitor from the country say, "it contains a large number of very interesting works." I know it was not right, and hope the Museum authorities will not be severe upon me if any of them reads this confession; but I wanted a desk, and set myself to consider which of the many very interesting works which a grateful nation places at the disposal of its would-be authors was best suited for my purpose.

For mere reading I suppose one book is pretty much as good as another; but the choice of a desk-book is a more serious matter. It must be neither too thick nor too thin; it must be large enough to make a substantial support; it must be strongly bound so as not to yield or give; it must not be too troublesome to carry backwards and forwards; and it must live on shelf C, D, or E, so that there need be no stooping or reaching too high. These are the conditions which a really good book must fulfil; simple, however, as they are, it is surprising how few volumes comply with them satisfactorily; moreover, being perhaps too sensitively conscientious, I allowed another consideration to influence me, and was sincerely anxious not to take a book which would be in constant use for reference by readers, more especially as, if I did this, I might find myself disturbed by the officials.

For weeks I made experiments upon sundry poetical and philosophical works, whose names I have forgotten, but could not succeed in finding my ideal desk, until at length, more by luck than cunning, I happened to light upon Frost's *Lives of Eminent Christians*, which I had no sooner tried than I discovered it to be the very perfection and *ne plus ultra* of everything that a book should be. It lived in Case No. 2008, and I accordingly took at once to sitting in Row B, where for the last dozen years or so I have sat ever since.

The first thing I have done whenever I went to the Museum has been to take down Frost's *Lives of Eminent Christians* and carry it to my seat. It is not the custom of modern writers to refer to the works to which they are most deeply indebted, and I have never, that I remember, mentioned it by name before; but it is to this book alone that I have looked for support during many years of literary labour, and it is round this to me invaluable volume that all my own have page by page grown up. There is none in the Museum to which I have been under anything like such constant obligation, none which I can so ill spare, and none which I would choose so readily if I were allowed to select one single volume and keep it for my own.

Note. This passage, which comes from an essay by Samuel Butler (1835–1902), had to be longer than most others because it takes somewhat longer to make its chief points clear. The title of the essay, *Quis Desiderio . . . ?* comes from the *Odes* of Horace and the whole sentence may be translated 'Why blush at our regret for the loss of such a dear friend?' The British Museum Reading Room is an enormous circular room, lined with books of reference, in which serious students may work. In the middle of the room is the catalogue, in hundreds of volumes, which contains the titles of the immense majority of all printed books. Books from the open shelves may be used by students, but most books must be ordered from the catalogue and are obtained by attendants from other parts of the library.

1. Read the passage through, aloud if possible, and make a first attempt to say in what 'tone of voice' you think it is written. You may want to modify this later when you have looked at details.

2. The opening paragraph of the essay explains the occasion for writing it. Express this occasion in your own words. Why is the title of the magazine appropriate in the author's view? In the phrase "(I) went to the British Museum to see what books I had written" he means that he went to consult the big catalogue of all printed books. Explain the joke here. What does he mean by "I was about to try and diminish the large and ever-increasing

circle of my non-readers"? How could this circle increase? Why does he say it in so roundabout a way?

3. What evidence in paragraph two can you find that Butler shares the contemporary interest in biological theories? What is the joke about the country visitor's remark?

4. What sort of humour is illustrated by paragraph three? Explain the irony of the opening sentence. How do you suppose the reference books are arranged? How are the shelves lettered? What elements in the tone and the content of paragraph three lead on to the next paragraph?

5. What is Butler's real attitude to Frost's book? How does he make this clear?

6. Point out two puns in the last paragraph and explain them—*i.e.*, show (*a*) what he appears to mean (*b*) what he really means by them.

7. The passage goes on to say that Frost's book is missing when he goes for it, and it is this that "bids fair . . . to put an end to my literary existence altogether." Wherein lies the irony of the last sentence in the passage?

8. Reconsider Question 1. What sort of writing can we call this? What is its purpose? Is it effective? How intelligent does it presuppose its audience to be? Why is such writing more effective if the writer 'keeps a straight face'?

(IV)

Travel, in the younger sort, is a part of education; in the elder, a part of experience. He that travelleth into a country, before he hath some entrance into the language, goeth to school and not to travel. That young man travel under some tutor or grave servant, I allow well; so that he be such a one that hath the language and hath been in the country before; whereby he may be able to tell them what things are worthy to be seen in the country where they go; what acquaintances they are to seek, what exercises or discipline the place yieldeth. For else young men shall go hooded and look abroad little.

It is a strange thing that in sea voyages, where there is nothing to be seen but sky and sea, men should make diaries; but in land travel, wherein so much is to be observed, for the most part they omit it; as if chance were fitter to be registered than observation. Let diaries, therefore, be brought in use.

The things to be seen and observed are:—the courts of princes, specially when they give audience to ambassadors; the courts of justice, while they sit and hear causes, and so of consistories ecclesiastic; the churches and monasteries, with the monuments which are therein extant; the walls and fortifications of cities and towns, and so the havens and harbours; antiquities and ruins: libraries, colleges, disputations and lectures, where any are; shipping and navies; houses and gardens of state and pleasure near great cities; armories; arsenals; magazines; exchanges; burses; warehouses; exercises of horsemanship; fencing; training of soldiers and the like; comedies, such whereunto the better sort of persons do resort; treasuries of jewels and robes; cabinets and rarities; and, to conclude, whatsoever is memorable in the places where they go. After all which the tutors or servants ought to make diligent enquiry. As for triumphs, masques, feasts, weddings, funerals, capital executions and such shews, men need not to be put in mind of them; yet are they not to be neglected.

If you will have a young man to put his travel into a little room, and in short time to gather much, this you must do. First, as was said, he must have some entrance into the language before he goeth. Then he must have such a servant or tutor, as knoweth the country, as was likewise said. Let him carry with him also some card or book describing the country where he travelleth; which will be a good key to his enquiry. Let him keep also a diary. Let him not stay long in one city or town; more or less as the place deserveth, but not long: nay, when he stayeth in one city or town, let him change his lodging from one end and part of the town to another; which is a great adamant of acquaintance. Let him sequester himself from the company of his companion, and diet in such places where there is good company of the nation where he travelleth.

1. This is part of one of Francis Bacons' celebrated essays, entitled *Of Travel*, and was first published in 1625. Read the passage through and then summarize, in a sentence each, the main topics of the four paragraphs printed.

2. Consider the language of the opening paragraph. What is meant by the opening generalization? What does "the younger *sort*" mean? In what sense is travel a part of education? Is it equally true now? Is it an essential part? For whom? What is the meaning of the second sentence, particularly of "goeth to school"?

3. Explain "I *allow* well." What are the advantages of taking a tutor? What is meant by "what *exercises* or *discipline* the place yieldeth"? "Hooded" is a metaphor taken from falconry: what does it mean here?

4. Bacon says that sea voyages are often recorded in diary form, but land travel less often. Can you suggest any reason why? What is meant by "as if chance were fitter to be registered than observation"?

5. What change of topic occurs at the beginning of the third paragraph? Account for the general range of "things to be seen" that Bacon recommends. What kind of young man has he particularly in mind? What three institutions does he recommend observing in special circumstances ("consistories" are ecclesiastical courts)? Suggest modern words for "exchanges" and "burses." What reservation does Bacon make about "comedies," and why? "Cabinets" are museums. How does Bacon summarize his advice on what to see abroad? Explain the last sentence of the paragraph, particularly "men need not be put in mind of them." What seems particularly odd to a modern ear in this last sentence?

6. Explain the metaphor which opens the last paragraph, about putting travel "into a little room." Paraphrase "he must have some entrance into the language." What do you think a "card" is (French 'carte')? What is the purpose of moving his lodgings from one end of the town to the other ("adamant" is a magnet)? Paraphrase "let him sequester himself from the company of his countrymen." Is this good advice? Is it relevant nowadays?

7. Who is envisaged as the reader of this essay? Is it the young man himself? Make some general comments on the style and consider this judgment about the *Essays*: "They are unequalled for their conciseness, their pertinence, their practical suggestiveness, their vivacity, even when treating of trite subjects, and their compression of many thoughts into the smallest possible compass in words." Could you write a satisfactory précis of this passage, in say, a third of the original number of words? Where does he use learned and common language side by side? Point out some examples of antithesis or balance in the sentence structure. Is the style pithy, urbane, pompous, vigorous, verbose? Is the manner self-assured, moralizing, didactic? Does the writer show any real distinction of mind, or is he merely summarizing the obvious?

(V)

In the first row, then, of the first gallery did Mr Jones, Mrs Miller, her youngest daughter and Partridge take their places. Partridge immediately declared it was the finest place he had ever been in. When the first music was played, he said it was a wonder how so many fiddlers could play at one time without putting one another out. While the fellow was lighting the upper candles, he cried out to Mrs Miller, "Look, look, madam, the very picture of the man in the end of the Common Prayer Book before the gunpowder-treason service." Nor could he help observing with a sigh, when all the candles were lighted, that here were candles enow burnt in one night to keep an honest poor family for a whole twelvemonth.

As soon as the play, which was *Hamlet, Prince of Denmark*, began, Partridge was all attention, nor did he break silence till the entrance of the ghost; upon which he asked Jones, what man that was in the strange dress, "something," said he, "like what I have seen in a picture. Sure it is not armour, is it?" Jones answered, "That is the ghost." To which Partridge replied with a smile, "Persuade me to that, sir, if you can. Though I can't say I ever actually saw a ghost in my life, yet I am certain I should know one if I saw him better than that comes to. No, no, sir, ghosts don't appear in such dresses as that, neither." In this mistake, which caused much laughter in the neighbourhood of Partridge, he was suffered to continue till the scene between the ghost and Hamlet, when Partridge gave that credit to Mr Garrick which he had denied to Jones, and fell into so violent a trembling that his knees knocked against each other. Jones asked him what was the matter, and whether he was afraid of the warrior upon the stage, "O la, sir!" said he, "I perceive now it is what you told me. I am not afraid of anything, for I know it is but a play; and if it was really a ghost, it could do one no harm at such a distance and in so much company; and yet, if I was frightened, I am not the only person."—"Why, who," cries Jones, "dost thou take to be such a coward here besides thyself?"—"Nay, you may call me coward if you will; but if that little man there upon the stage is not frightened, I never saw any man frightened in my life. Ay, ay; go along with you! Ay, to be sure! Who's fool then? Will you? Lud have mercy upon such foolhardiness! Whatever happens, it is good enough for you. Follow you? I'd follow the devil as soon. Nay, perhaps it is the devil; for they say he can put on what likeness he pleases. Oh, here he is again! No farther, no, you have gone far enough already —farther than I'd have gone for all the king's dominions." Jones offered to speak, but Partridge cried, "Hush, hush, dear sir! don't you hear him?" And during the whole speech of the ghost he sat with his eyes fixed partly on the ghost and partly on Hamlet, and with his mouth open: the same passions, which succeeded each other in Hamlet, succeeded likewise in him.

When the scene was over, Jones said, "Why, Partridge, you exceed my expectations. You enjoy the play more than I conceived possible."—"Nay, sir," answered Partridge, "if you are not afraid of the devil, I can't help it: but to be sure it is natural to be surprised at such things, though I know there is nothing in them: not that it was the ghost that surprised me neither, for I should have known that to have been only a man in a strange dress; but when I saw the little man so frightened himself, it was that which took hold of me."—"And dost thou imagine, then, Partridge," cried Jones, "that he was really frightened?"—"Nay, sir," said Partridge, "did not you yourself observe afterwards, when he found it was his own father's spirit, and how he was murdered in the garden, how his fear forsook him by degrees, and he was struck dumb with sorrow, as it were, just as I should have been had it been my own case?"

Note. This passage comes towards the end of Henry Fielding's vast novel, *Tom Jones,* which was first published in 1748. Partridge is Tom's companion and servant, an odd mixture of learning and complete naivety. The performance they attend at the theatre is of Shakespeare's *Hamlet* with David Garrick, a contemporary of Fielding's and most famous of English actors, in the title-rôle.

1. What are Partidge's reactions to the theatre before the performance begins? What indication of character and background do they provide? Do you think he has been to a theatre before?

2. Partridge refuses to believe in the ghost, but on the wrong grounds. What exactly is "this mistake" which caused much laughter in the neighbourhood of Partridge?

3. At what point does Partridge begin to feel frightened of the ghost? What is meant by saying that "he gave that credit to Mr Garrick which he had denied to Jones"? Why is Garrick referred to as "*Mr* Garrick"? Who is "the warrior upon the stage"?

4. In the speech which begins "O la, sir!" where does Partridge contradict himself? What actions contradict his

statements? What comfort does he gain from being at some distance from the stage? How does he defend his fear?

5. "If that little man upon the stage is not frightened, I never saw any man frightened in my life" (Garrick was small of stature). What does Partridge mean by this statement? Where is the joke? What light does it cast on Garrick's performance? What is meant by "Ay, ay, go along with you!" and "Follow you? I'd follow the devil as soon." (You may need to look at the relevant scenes in the play.)

6. What is meant by "Jones *offered* to speak"? Why does Partridge quieten him? (The speech of the ghost referred to here is quoted elsewhere in this book—p. 198). Consider the last sentence in this paragraph ("And during the whole speech . . .") and say what rôle it plays in the paragraph. What does it suggest about the comparative acting skill of the ghost and of Hamlet? What does it tell us (*a*) of Garrick (*b*) of Partridge?

7. What irony is there in Jones' comment to Partridge when the scene is over? Is there a sense in which Partridge *can* be said to have enjoyed the play?

8. Where does Partidge describe the progress of the scene, and in terms of whose reactions? Is there *any* sense in "when I saw the little man so frightened, it was that which took hold of me"? (This may involve you in considering the various factors which cause fear.) Later on he says of Claudius, Hamlet's father-in-law who killed his brother, "Who would think, by looking in the king's face, that he had ever committed a murder?" What is amusing about this? What confusion between reality and stage illusion does he show in these two statements? Does the latter praise the actor by implication?

9. Before they set out for the theatre, we are told that Jones "expected to enjoy much entertainment in the criticisms of Partridge, from whom he expected the simple dictates of nature, unimproved, indeed, but likewise unadulterated by art." Explain this and illustrate it from the passage. What does "art" mean here? Is there *any* sense in which Partridge has advantages, as a spectator, over his more sophisticated companions?

10. Is Jones fond of Partridge? Contemptuous? Both? Is Partridge merely a fool? Is his inexperience at all a source of strength? Does he cast any light on the drama or acting? How does he compare as a comic character with Dogberry? (see p. 196). Write a comment on the style of this passage. Does it strike you as strong and 'masculine,' a word frequently used to commend Fielding's style?

(VI)

I left in a French steamer, and she called in every blamed port they have out there, for, as far as I could see, the sole purpose of landing soldiers and custom-house officers. I watched the coast. Watching a coast as it slips by the ship is like thinking about an enigma. There it is before you—smiling, frowning, inviting, grand, mean, insipid, or savage, and always mute with an air of whispering. Come and find out. This one was almost featureless, as if still in the making, with an aspect of monotonous grimness. The edge of a colossal jungle, so dark-green as to be almost black, fringed with white surf, ran straight, like a ruled line, far, far away along a blue sea whose glitter was blurred by a creeping mist. The sun was fierce, the land seemed to glisten and drip with steam. Here and there grayish-whitish specks showed up clustered inside the white surf, with a flag flying above them perhaps. Settlements some centuries old, and still no bigger than pin-heads on the untouched expanse of their background. We pounded along, stopped, landed soldiers; went on, landed custom-house clerks to levy toll in what looked like a God-forsaken wilderness, with a tin shed and a flag-pole lost in it; landed more soldiers—to take care of the custom-house clerks, presumably. Some, I heard, got drowned in the surf; but whether they did or not, nobody seemed particularly to care. They were just flung out there, and on we went. Every day the coast looked the same, as though we had not moved;

but we passed various places—trading places—with names like Gran' Bassam, Little Popo; names that seemed to belong to some sordid farce acted in front of a sinister back-cloth. The idleness of a passenger, my isolation amongst all these men with whom I had no point of contact, the oily and languid sea, the uniform sombreness of the coast, seemed to keep me away from the truth of things, within the toil of a mournful and senseless delusion. The voice of the surf heard now and then was a positive pleasure, like the speech of a brother. It was something natural, that had its reason, that had a meaning. Now and then a boat from the shore gave one a momentary contact with reality. It was paddled by black fellows. You could see from afar the white of their eyeballs glistening. They shouted, sang; their bodies streamed with perspiration; they had faces like grotesque masks—these chaps; but they had bone, muscle, a wild vitality, an intense energy of movement, that was as natural and true as the surf along their coast. They wanted no excuse for being there. They were a great comfort to look at. For a time I would feel I belonged still to a world of straight-forward facts; but the feeling would not last long. Something would turn up to scare it away. Once, I remember we came upon a man-of-war anchored off the coast. There wasn't even a shed there, and she was shelling the bush. It appears the French had one of their wars going on thereabouts. Her ensign dropped limp like a rag; the muzzles of the long six-inch guns stuck out all over the low hull; the greasy, slimy swell swung her up lazily and let her down, swaying her thin masts. In the empty immensity of earth, sky and water, there she was, incomprehensible, firing into a continent. Pop, would go one of the six-inch guns; a small flame would dart and vanish, a little white smoke would disappear, a tiny projectile would give a feeble screech—and nothing happened. Nothing could happen. There was a touch of insanity in the proceeding, a sense of lugubrious drollery in the sight; and it was not dissipated by somebody on board assuring me earnestly there was a camp of natives—he called them enemies!—hidden out of sight somewhere.

1. This passage comes from *The Heart of Darkness*, one of Joseph Conrad's 'long short stories,' about one-third the length of a novel, and was first published in 1902. The narrator of this, and of several other stories, is a middle-aged sailor called Marlow. It describes part of a journey into Africa where he is taking up a post as agent for a trading company. Point out some elements in this passage which show that it is spoken narrative.

2. The coast he is passing is described as "almost featureless." Quote some other expressions which echo this one; and then show how he makes his description of this featureless coast interesting. How can it be "mute with an air of *whispering*"?

3. Where are colour-adjectives used? Where is the sea itself described? What is the significance of the following sentence: "Settlements some centuries old, and still no bigger than pinheads on the untouched expanse of their background"?

4. "Names that seemed to belong to some sordid farce acted in front of a sinister back-cloth." What elements of farce have already been shown? What is the "sinister back-cloth"? What kept Marlow "within the toil of a mournful and senseless delusion"? What does "toil" mean here?

5. What is contrasted implicitly with "the voice of the surf"? In what sense did a boat from the shore give one "a momentary contact with reality"? What does he emphasize in his description of the African boatmen? Why were they "a great comfort to look at"?

6. What rôle is played by the story about the man-of-war? Pay particular attention to these expressions: "she was shelling the bush," "the French had one of their wars going on thereabouts," "the ensign dropped limp like a rag," "firing into a continent." What attitude is shown by the italicized words in this sentence: "*Pop*, would go one of the six-inch guns; a *small* flame would dart and vanish, a *little* white smoke would disappear, a *tiny* projectile would give a *feeble* screech—and *nothing happened*"? Does a six-inch gun fire a "tiny" projectile? Explain "lugubrious drollery" and the expression within dashes "he called them enemies!" Why the exclamation mark?

7. What features of this passage suggest the immensity and

mysteriousness of the coast? In contrast, what features describe the efforts of civilization to tame this continent? How is its failure shown? Is the attitude to "civilization" cynical? What attitude to French colonialism is implied?

8. Compare this passage with other descriptive writing about the tropics that you have read. What, essentially, is the difference? A critic has said of the stories told through the mind and mouth of Marlow: "Further, Marlow, slow and ruminative, served to hold back Conrad's poetic urgency, and by laconically dealing out the tale piecemeal, also kept it to earth." Does the passage quoted confirm this statement?

9. Conrad was a Pole who did not even learn English until his twenties. Can you detect that this is the writing of a foreigner? What two kinds of experience make up the main content of the passage, and does the author use a distinct style for these two 'sides'? Attempt an evaluation of the style of the passage. Is it over-written, dignified, 'romantic,' natural, brilliant, subtle, vigorous, noble? Is the response required simple or complex?

Chapter Ten

SOME PASSAGES FOR COMPARISON

THIS chapter offers some poems and passages for direct comparison. I have left this till last in the book, because the task of comparison demands some experience in examining single passages, and only after a fair amount of practice in close reading are we likely to have the equipment needed to deal with two passages, first separately and then, as it were, simultaneously.

The passages have been chosen because of some relation between them, but this relation must not be assumed to be the same in each case. They may relate in time or subject-matter; they may show constrasting casts of mind dealing with similar problems. Certainly the task of comparison should not be thought of solely in terms of 'spotting the winner,' though the process of evaluation will often drive us to a conclusion as to which is the better passage. Here, as everywhere else, there is no substitute for close reading.

I have started by making a detailed comparison between two poems, which are closely related in period and subject-matter. This is followed by six pairs of passages for the student to compare. The first consists of two free translations from the same Latin poem; the second of two prose passages concerned with gardens; the third puts side by side a serious poem and a parody of it; the fourth offers two poems similar in general mood, subject, and period, but with differences in thought; the fifth consists of two descriptive passages by fairly recent writers, which again show radical differences in their attitudes; and the last gives two prologues to plays.

No detailed questions are asked on these passages, because the student should by now be able to ask his own, and because they would give too clear a lead; but a sentence or two suggests how they might be approached.

(*a*) *The Soldier*

If I should die, think only this of me:
  That there's some corner of a foreign field
That is for ever England. There shall be
  In that rich earth a richer dust concealed;
A dust whom England bore, shaped, made aware,
  Gave once her flowers to love, her ways to roam,
A body of England's, breathing English air,
  Washed by the rivers, blest by suns of home.

And think, this heart, all evil shed away,
  A pulse in the eternal mind, no less
  Gives somewhere back the thoughts by England given;
Her sights and sounds; dreams happy as her day;
  And laughter, learnt of friends; and gentleness,
    In hearts at peace, under an English heaven.

RUPERT BROOKE

(*b*) *Anthem for Doomed Youth*

What passing-bells for those who die as cattle?
  Only the monstrous anger of the guns.
  Only the stuttering rifles' rapid rattle
Can patter out their hasty orisons.
No mockeries for them from prayers or bells,
  Nor any voice of mourning save the choirs—
The shrill, demented choirs of wailing shells;
  And bugles calling for them from sad shires.

What candles may be held to speed them all?
  Not in the hands of boys, but in their eyes
Shall shine the holy glimmers of good-byes.
  The pallor of girls' brows shall be their pall;
Their flowers the tenderness of silent minds,
And each slow dusk a drawing-down of blinds.

WILFRED OWEN

These two poems offer themselves for comparison as they were both written during and about the First World War, they are similar in length and form (both are sonnets), and they were both (incidentally) written by young poets who died during that war.

We may start by reading the two sonnets through, first silently, and then aloud. It is not essential to know anything about the structure of a sonnet, but for convenience we shall want to use the terms *octave* and *sestet* and must therefore explain them. Most sonnets consist of fourteen lines and divide into a group of eight lines, generally consisting of two quatrains (four lines) marked off by rhyme and often also by punctuation, which is called the *octave*; and a group of six lines (variously divided into two threes, three twos, or a four and a two) called the *sestet*. There is commonly a strong break in content or direction between octave and sestet, though this is not very marked in the first (as we shall see) and rather stronger in the second.

One of the earliest impressions we are likely to form is that the first sonnet consists of three sentences only, one ending at "England" in the middle of the third line, the next running to the end of the octave, and the third occupying the whole of the sestet. The dominant punctuation is the semi-colon, and the sentences move *across* the rhythmic and rhyme scheme. The second sonnet, in contrast to this, tends to use the quatrain, the couplet, or even the single line, as a unit of thought. To put it in another way, there is a tendency in the first poem to 'run on,' and in the second to 'end-stop': the lines are units in the second, parts of sentences in the first. This may seem a trifling difference to put so early in our analysis, but it will be found relevant, if not essential, to the total effect.[1]

To move from structural aspects to questions of content (these two are not, of course, really separable, and are only treated as such for convenience), one of the things we notice early is that in the first sonnet the war is seen in personal terms, in the second much more impersonally. The first starts with "If *I* should die, think only this of *me*," the second "What passing-bells for *those* who die as cattle?" The word "I" would be entirely out of place in the second sonnet. And although the first person singular is not again used in the first poem, the subject remains the same: "a richer dust," in apposition to "a body of England's," and "this heart" are the subjects of the other two sentences, and they are both aspects of the "I" of the first one. Parallel to this is the observation that the first sonnet sees the war solely in English terms (the word "England" or "English" occurs six times), while the second could in the main apply to either side in the war, but at least applies, as the title shows, to the whole of the English army and not only to one member of it. Moreover, in the first poem the subject ("I") embodies or contains all the aspects of England which the rest of the poem deals with, while the second sees imaginatively the fate of the whole youth of England, or Europe.

We now move on to the question of tone—which is determined largely by vocabulary and rhythm. In the first poem the rhythms are flaccid in the first half of both octave

[1] See the discussion (p. 97) of Keats' *To Autumn* for another example where grammatical' structure is of importance.

and sestet, and jerky in the catalogues which follow. Nowhere is rhythm or sound used for any more precise purpose than evoking a tepid sentiment. The poet starts by asking the reader to realize that if he dies he will have left his own body to enrich "some corner of a foreign field." The "dust" is his own body, or what remains of it, and it was born, nurtured and educated in England. The sestet deals with his heart, which will have lost all evil in the cleansing process of death, and will still be able to evoke all the associations of pre-war England. At the critical points here, and both in the octave and the sestet, there is a lack of definition, so that we are not quite sure what is meant. "Gives *somewhere* back the thoughts by England given" is the critical line in the sestet and contains the main verb; but the word "somewhere" is a confession of failure and expresses a vague and undefined hope rather than any sort of conviction. Similarly in the octave, the "richer dust" is the critical point and this, too, raises more problems than it solves. In what sense "richer"? Because it is human, rather than animal or plant? 'Because it is English' seems to be implied—in which case we are driven perilously near the absurd idea that English corpses make better compost than those of foreigners. If he means simply 'human,' then he can claim no uniqueness for his "richer dust": a poet should have enough imagination to realize that a French or German or Italian soldier has for him an equally rich background of association, and his body will therefore, in this sense, produce an equally rich dust. This seems like a piece of false particularization. The rest of the poem (lines 5 to 8 of the octave and lines 12 to 14 of the sestet) can be shown to be little more than catalogues, the first divided by commas, the second by semi-colons, presumably to slow down the movement. The catalogues may seem 'poetic' because they offer the standard poetic words: "flowers," "blest," "dreams," "gentleness," "peace," "heaven," all linked together by a continual repetition of the words "English" and "England", which, in this kind of writing and at the beginning of a great war, seem the most poetic words of all: and indeed, they may be so used provided it is remembered that 'Yugo-Slav' or 'Rumanian' is equally 'poetic' for Yugo-Slavs and Rumanians.

It should now be possible to evaluate the first poem. It starts with an egoistic line masquerading as modesty. If this is felt to be unfair, the next line and a half bears it out. *His* body will make some corner of a foreign field *for ever* England: this seems a large claim. The "richer dust" represents, as we have tried to show, either a monstrous egotism or a blinkered nationalism; and we go on to a catalogue, in the most general terms, of how England gave this body her flowers, her "ways" ('poetic' for 'roads'), how it breathed the air of England, bathed in its rivers, and was blessed by its sun. Two comments may be added here: "A body of England's" is the most blatant repetition of what has already been twice said, which adds nothing and appears merely to fill up the line; and secondly, though we can think of English rivers and flowers and even air as different from any other, it is a little absurd to speak of an English sun.

Having said "think *only* this," the poet asks more of us—"And think," which suggests that he doesn't really mean "only." This heart is no less than a pulse in the eternal mind; what this means is not apparent. It certainly doesn't sound modest, and may mean that after death all souls revert to the heaven from whence they came: but how can a *heart* be a *pulse* in a *mind*? Something has already been said about "somewhere"; the heart now gives back the "thoughts by England given." How hearts give back thoughts is not revealed, but perhaps more surprising is that the thoughts listed in the second catalogue, which follows, are not thoughts at all. Is "laughter" a thought? Is "gentleness"? Are "sights" or "sounds" or "dreams"? The "hearts at peace" may be his friends and himself in the years before the war, or the expression may anticipate the years of peace that are to follow, or it may simply mean that anyone would be at peace in such surroundings or that they are dead. In any case the last line with its four 'stock-response' words—"hearts," "peace," "English," "heaven" is more or less guaranteed to ring the bell; and by now one feels sour enough to point out that, not satisfied with nationalizing the sun, the poet now wishes to monopolize heaven itself.

The second poem considers the traditional rituals of death and tries to discover whether they could be appropriate to the "doomed youth." The opening line sets the tone of the whole octave. "Passing-bells" are rung in the church when some one has died, to register his "passing"; and the expression evokes a whole way of life, in a decent ordered community where death is viewed with respect and decorum. How could such a ritual be appropriate to the thousands who are dying now? The contrast between the "passing bells" and "those who die as cattle" shows the clash at its most complete. That ancient and beautiful way of life is finished: the battle-line is a slaughterhouse. Instead of the quiet tolling of the bell they have "Only the monstrous anger of the guns . . . Only the stuttering rifles' rapid rattle . . ." The first of these lines with its round vowels in "monstrous" "anger," "guns," suggests the huge open mouths of the gun muzzles and the devastating noise as they fire. In contrast the line about rifles gives in its rhythm, its sharp consonants, its alliteration on '*r*' and '*t*', and its repeated sound in "rapid," "rattle," and "pattern" in the next line, the very sound of staccato rifle-fire. "Orisons" are prayers;

the word is archaic Anglo-French, and again conjures up a similar set of associations to that of "passing-bells," but "orisons" would be slow and dignified and "hasty orisons" is a contradiction in terms, which shows that the word "orisons" is used ironically. To call the gunfire an orison is a mockery, as the poet says in the next line; to pretend that this sort of death (those who die as cattle) is dignified or quiet is to mock it. The dead can expect no mourning except from "choirs"; the word again evokes a peace-time funeral service—but there is a dash after the word, which is also used ironically; they can expect only the high-pitched "singing" of the shells ("shrill, demented") as they shriek through the air. The last line is an exquisite modulation to the gentle and delicate movement of the sestet—itself the equivalent of the peace that death brings, however savage the mode of death. The whole poem quietens down in this line. The bugles are those that were blown when these young men were training in England: most infantry regiments were recruited on a county basis and training camps were set up in the counties. Thus the soldier's last memories of England would be of these camps, and the bugles which woke them and became associated with their last few weeks in England. The regiments would often be called by the name of the county (the Leicestershire Regiment, the Hampshire Regiment) and "sad shires" with its slow rhythm therefore exactly gives the poignant feeling of the county which has lost so many of its young men, of the wives and children left behind, of the regiment itself which blows the "Last Post" on the bugle for its own dead.

The sestet continues with the ritual imagery of death: "What candles may be held to speed them all?" echoes the opening question of the poem, and "to speed" means 'to bid godspeed,' that is, to say farewell to the dead and speed them on their journey to heaven. They can have no candles for their funeral service, but the glitter of tears in their comrades' eyes will act as a substitute. The beautiful modulation

> Not in the hands of boys, but in their eyes

moves the image from candles held by choirboys in a funeral procession to the eyes of the other "boys," those who are no more than boys, who carry their bodies or learn of their death; and the glimmer is equally "holy" in each case. The "pall" is a cloth spread over a coffin; the "pallor" or paleness of their mourning sweethearts is identified with this by means of a pun. Flowers are usual at funerals, but the only flowers they can hope for are those flowers of the spirit that come from the tender memories of those they have left behind. The last line is a triumph of compression. Blinds were drawn down to indicate that some one in the house had died and to show respect for the dead: here nature itself 'draws the blinds' each day at dusk in sympathy for the death of those thousands of men.

If these analyses are accepted, the implicit comparison can be made explicit in very little space. It is interesting, though not essential, to know that the first sonnet was written within a few months of the beginning of the war by Rupert Brooke, who died in the Aegean a year later; while the second was written by Wilfred Owen after the war had dragged on more and more hideously for over two years; and it may be that the essentially 'romantic,' subjective, and nationalistic flavour of the first was only possible when men did not know what war really meant, while the savage disillusion of the second reflects the only possible reaction after the Marne and the Somme and the holocausts of those two years. But this information only endorses a judgment that can be affirmed in purely critical terms, of the poems as poems. The first is loosely constructed, sprawling in its sentence structure, repetitive, and unrealized—that is, the poet has large loose ideas which he has not brought into focus in the poem itself; the second is taut, concentrated, a 'continuum.' The first uses words vaguely, as evocative counters: the second with extreme precision, as units in a sequence of individual thought and individual feeling. The first uses sound and rhythms diffusely and the pace is not varied except, apparently, by accident; the second shows an intense awareness of sound and can vary it for particular purposes, echoing its meanings constantly with the sounds expressing them. The first has little real imagery: the second is rich with images, each of which adds its quota to the total effect. The first relies on such un-worked-out generalities as "richer dust" and "a pulse in the eternal mind": the second is always specific. The first offers a generalized string of faint evocations and a very simple pattern of concept and thought: the second is by comparison extremely complex, sensitive, and deeply felt. The first asks us to make a number of easy 'penny-in-the-slot' responses: the second rejects all that is 'sweet' and 'easy' and requires of us a new effort of the mind and the imagination. The first is self-centred, the second compassionate. The first hurls the word "English" at us over and over again, with the implication that the war itself is somehow glamorous: the second goes beyond personal or national boundaries, and sees the horror and cruelty of war, and can modulate from a savage hatred to a delicate pity. The second poem has, I believe, some weaknesses (there is a certain diffusion about the last line but one, and the pun ('pallor-pall') doesn't seem entirely defensible) but in comparison with the first it is a triumph of organization and behind it is a mind of far greater distinction. There can be little question as to which poem better stands up to a close examination.

(I)

(a) Vivamus mea Lesbia atque amemus

My sweetest Lesbia, let us live and love;
And though the sager sort our deeds reprove,
Let us not weigh them. Heaven's great lamps do dive
Into their west, and straight again revive;
But, soon as once set is our little light,
Then must we sleep one ever-during night.

If all would lead their lives in love like me,
Then bloody swords and armour should not be;
No drum nor trumpet peaceful sleeps should move,
Unless alarm came from the camp of Love.
But fools do live and waste their little light,
And seek with pain their ever-during night.

When timely death my life and fortunes ends,
Let not my hearse be vext with mourning friends;
But let all lovers rich in triumph come,
And with sweet pastime grace my happy tomb.
And, Lesbia, close up thou my little light,
And crown with love my ever-during night.

THOMAS CAMPION

(b) Vivamus mea Lesbia atque amemus

Come, my Celia, let us prove,
While we can, the sports of love.
Time will not be ours for ever;
He, at length, our good will sever.
Spend not then his gifts in vain:
Suns that set may rise again.
But if once we lose this light,
'Tis with us perpetual night.

Why should we defer our joys?
Fame and rumour are but toys.
Cannot we delude the eyes
Of a few poor household spies?
Or his easier ears beguile,
Thus removèd by our wile?
'Tis no sin love's fruits to steal,
But the sweet thefts to reveal;
To be taken, to be seen,
These have crimes accounted been.

BEN JONSON

These are both free translations of Catullus' famous poem by poets who were nearly contemporaries. The text of the original poem is given below to save trouble in finding it, but it is by no means essential to read or study this, as the two poems have an independent existence and both can be said to be inspired by the original lines rather than to give renderings of them. Latin is therefore not necessary, and if students have no Latin the exercise can still be done. The poems should be compared as treatments of a similar mood.

Vivamus, mea Lesbia, atque amemus,
rumoresque senum severiorum
omnes unius aestimemus assis.
soles occidere et redire possunt:
nobis cum semel occidit brevis lux,
nox est perpetua una dormienda.
da mi basia mille, deinde centum,
dein mille altera, dein secunda centum,
deinde usque altera mille, deinde centum.
dein, cum milia multa fecerimus,
conturbabimus illa, ne sciamus,
aut nequis malus invidere possit,
cum tantum sciat esse basiorum.

(II)

(*a*)

Because I take the garden I have named to have been in all kinds the most beautiful and perfect, at least in the figure and disposition, that I have ever seen, I will describe it for a model to those that meet with such a situation, and are above the regards of common expense. It lies on the side of a hill (upon which the house stands), but not very steep. The length of the house, where the best rooms are of most use or pleasure are, lies upon the breadth of the garden; the great parlour opens into the middle of a terrace gravel walk that lies even with it, and which may be, as I remember, about three hundred paces long, and broad in proportion; the border set with standard laurels, and at large distances, which have the beauty of orange-trees out of flower and fruit: from this walk are three descents by many stone steps, in the middle and at each end, into a very large parterre. This is divided into quarters by gravel walks, and adorned by two fountains and eight statues in the several quarters; at the end of the terrace walk are two summer-houses, and the sides of the parterre are ranged with two large cloisters, open to the garden, upon arches of stone, and ending with two other summer-houses even with the cloisters, which are paved with stone, and designed for walks of shade, there being none other in the whole parterre. Over these two cloisters are two terraces covered with lead and fenced with balusters; and the passage into these airy walks is out of the two summer-houses, at the end of the first terrace walk. The cloister facing the south is covered with vines, and would have been proper for an orange-house, and the other for myrtles, or other more common greens; and had, I doubt not, been cast for that purpose, if this piece of gardening had been then in as much vogue as it is now.

SIR WILLIAM TEMPLE

(*b*)

Adam walked by the rick-yard, at present empty of ricks, to the little wooden gate leading into the garden—once the well-tended kitchen-garden of a manor house; now, but for the handsome brick wall with stone coping that ran along one side of it, a true farmhouse garden, with hardy perennial flowers, unpruned fruit-trees, and kitchen vegetables growing together in careless, half-neglected abundance. In that leafy, flowery, bushy time, to look for any one in this garden was like playing at "hide-and-seek". There were the tall holly-hocks beginning to flower, and dazzle the eye with their pink, white and yellow; there were the syringas and gueldres roses, all large and disorderly for want of trimming; there were leafy walls of scarlet beans and late peas; there was a row of bushy filberts in one direction, and in another a huge apple-tree making a barren circle under its low-spreading boughs. But what signified a barren patch or two? The garden was so large. There was always a superfluity of broad beans—it took nine or ten of Adam's strides to get to the end of the uncut grass walk that ran by the side of them; and as for other vegetables, there was so much more room than was necessary for them, that in the rotation of crops a large flourishing bed of groundsel was of yearly occurrence on one spot or other. The very rose-trees, at which Adam stopped to pluck one, looked as if they grew wild; they were all huddled together in bushy masses, now flaunting with wide open petals, almost all of them of the streaked pink-and-white kind, which doubtless dated from the union of the houses of York and Lancaster. Adam was wise enough to choose a compact Provence rose that peeped out half-smothered by its flaunting scentless neighbours, and held it in his hand—he thought he should be more at ease holding something in his hand—as he walked on to the far end of the garden, where he remembered there was the largest row of currant-trees, not far off from the great yew-tree arbour.

George Eliot

The first passage is an extract from an essay on Moor Park Garden by Sir William Temple, the seventeenth-century essayist. The second passage comes from *Adam Bede* by George Eliot, the Victorian novelist. They can be compared as evocations of two different kinds of taste, shown by their subject-matter, and as two contrasting styles and 'tones of voice.'

(III)

(a)

She dwelt among the untrodden ways
  Beside the springs of Dove,
A Maid whom there were none to praise
  And very few to love:

A violet by a mossy stone
  Half hidden from the eye!
—Fair as a star, when only one
  Is shining in the sky.

She lived unknown, and few could know
  When Lucy ceased to be;
But she is in her grave, and, oh,
  The difference to me!

WILLIAM WORDSWORTH

(b)

He lived amidst th' untrodden ways
  To Rydal Lake that lead;
A bard whom there were none to praise,
  And very few to read.

Behind a cloud his mystic sense,
  Deep hidden, who can spy?
Bright as the night when not a star
  Is shining in the sky.

Unread his works—his "Milk White Doe"
  With dust is dark and dim;
It's still in Longmans' shop, and oh!
  The difference to him!

HARTLEY COLERIDGE

The first poem is one of the four celebrated short poems known as the 'Lucy' poems, and was written by Wordsworth in 1799. The parody was written by Hartley Coleridge, son of Wordsworth's close associate, S. T. Coleridge, during Wordsworth's lifetime, though it was not published until later. The student should consider whether the parody hits its target, whether it picks out real absurdities to mock or whether the original poem can stand up to the implicit attack and whether it is affectionate or cruel. This can lead on to a consideration of other examples of parodies, and what light they cast on the originals they mock. (A good source-book is *Apes and Parrots*, edited by Sir John Squire).

Note: Rydal Water was near Wordsworth's cottage; *The White Doe of Rylstone* is the title of one of his poems, and Longmans were his publishers.

(IV)

(*a*)

Fair Daffodils, we weep to see
  You haste away so soon;
As yet the early-rising sun
  Has not attained his noon.
      Stay, stay,
    Until the hasting day
      Has run

But to the even-song;
And, having prayed together, we
Will go with you along.

We have short time to stay, as you,
We have as short a spring;
As quick a growth to meet decay,
As you, or anything.
We die
As your hours do, and dry
Away,
Like to the summer's rain;
Or as the pearls of morning's dew,
Ne'er to be found again.

ROBERT HERRICK

(*b*)

I made a posie, while the day ran by:
Here will I smell my remnant out, and tie
My life within this band.
But Time did beckon to the flowers, and they
By noon most cunningly did steal away
And wither'd in my hand.

My hand was next to them, and then my heart:
I took, without more thinking, in good part
Time's gentle admonition:
Who did so sweetly death's sad taste convey,
Making my mind to smell my fatal day,
Yet sug'ring the suspicion.

Farewell, dear flowers, sweetly your time ye spent,
Fit, while ye liv'd, for smell or ornament,
And after death for cures.
I follow straight without complaints or grief,
Since, if my scent be good, I care not if
It be as short as yours.

GEORGE HERBERT

The two poems were written by contemporaries. Both are reflections on the quick blossoming and quick dying of flowers. The student should try to decide what the two poems have in common, how they differ, which is the more successful, and why.

(V)

(*a*)

The sun rose. Bars of yellow and green fell on the shore, gilding the ribs of the eaten-out boat and making the sea-holly and its mailed leaves gleam blue as steel. Light almost pierced the thin swift waves as they raced fan-shaped over the beach. The girl who had shaken her head and made all the jewels, the topaz, the aquamarine, the water-coloured jewels with sparks of fire in them, dance, now bared her brows and with wide-opened eyes drove a straight pathway over the waves. Their quivering mackerel sparkling was darkened; they massed themselves; their green hollows deepened and darkened and might be traversed by shoals of wandering fish. As they splashed and drew back they left a black rim of twigs and cork on the shore and straws and sticks of wood, as if some light shallop had foundered and burst its sides and the sailor had swum to land and bounded up the cliff and left his frail cargo to be washed ashore.

In the garden the birds that had sung erratically and spasmodically in the dawn on that tree, on that bush, now sang together in chorus, shrill and sharp; now together as if conscious of companionship, now alone as if to the pale blue sky. They swerved, all in one flight, when the black cat moved among the bushes, when the cook threw cinders on the ash heap and startled them. Fear was in their song, and apprehension of pain, and joy to be snatched quickly now at this instant. Also they sang emulously in the clear morning air, swerving high over the elm tree, singing together as they chased each other, escaping, pursuing, pecking each other as they turned high in the air. And then tiring of pursuit and flight, lovelily they came descending, delicately declining, dropped down and sat silent on the tree, on the wall, with their bright eyes glancing, and their heads turned this way, that way; aware, awake; intensely conscious of one thing, one object in particular.

Perhaps it was a snail shell, rising in the grass like a grey cathedral, a swelling building burnt with dark rings and shadowed green by the grass. Or perhaps they saw the splendour of the flowers making a light of flowing purple over the beds, through which dark tunnels of purple shade were driven between the stalks. Or they fixed their gaze on the small bright apple leaves, dancing yet withheld, stiffly sparkling among the pink-tipped blossoms. Or they saw the rain drop on the hedge, pendent but not falling, with a whole house bent in it, and towering elms; or, gazing straight at the sun, their eyes became gold beads.

VIRGINIA WOOLF

(*b*)

It was about two o'clock in the afternoon, one hot day in May, when Mr Polly, unhurrying and serene, came upon that broad bend of the river to which the little lawn and garden of the Potwell Inn run down. He stopped at the sight of the place and surveyed its deep tiled roof, nestling under big trees—you never get a decently big, decently shaped tree by the seaside—its sign towards the roadway, its sun-blistered green bench and tables, its shapely white windows and its row of upshooting hollyhock plants in the garden. A hedge separated the premises from a buttercup-yellow meadow, and beyond stood three poplars in a group against the sky, three exceptionally tall, graceful, and harmonious poplars. It is hard to say what there was about them that made them so beautiful to Mr Polly, but they seemed to him to touch a pleasant scene with a distinction almost divine. He stood admiring them quietly for a long time.

At last the need for coarser æsthetic satisfactions arose in him.

"Provinder," he whispered, drawing near to the inn. "Cold sirloin for choice. And nutbrown brew and wheaten bread."

The nearer he came to the place the more he liked it. The windows on the ground floor were long and low, and they had pleasing red blinds. The green tables outside were agreeably ringed with memories of former drinks, and an extensive grape vine spread level branches across the whole front of the place. Against the wall was a broken oar, two boat-hooks, and the stained and faded red cushions of a pleasure-boat. One went up three steps to the glass-panelled door, and peeped into a broad, low room with a bar and a beer-engine, behind which were many bright and helpful-looking bottles against mirrors, and great and little pewter measures, and bottles fastened in brass wire upside down, with their corks replaced by taps, and a white china cask labelled "Shrub," and cigar boxes, and boxes of cigarettes, and a couple of Toby jugs and a beautifully coloured hunting scene framed and glazed, showing the most elegant people taking Piper's Cherry Brandy, and cards such as the law requires about the dilution of spirits and the illegality of bringing children into bars, and satirical verses about swearing and asking for credit, and three very bright, red-cheeked wax apples, and a round-shaped clock.

H. G. WELLS

The first passage comes from a series of descriptive evocations which are interspersed in the narrative of Virginia Woolf's most famous novel *The Waves*. The second is from H. G. Wells' early novel *The History of Mr Polly*. Consider the aims of the two writers, how they select detail for their descriptions, and the kind of mind behind each passage.

(VI)

(*a*)

Now, luck yet send us, and a little wit
Will serve to make our play hit:
(According to the palates of the season)
Here is rhyme, not empty of reason.
This we were bid to credit, from our poet,
Whose true scope, if you would know it,
In all his poems still have been this measure,
To mix profit with your pleasure;
And not as some, whose throats their envy failing,
Cry hoarsely, All he writes is railing:
And when his plays come forth, think they can flout [them,
With saying, he was a year about them.
To this there needs no lie, but this his creature,
Which was, two months since, no feature;
And though he dares give them five lives to mend it,
'Tis known, five weeks fully penn'd it,
From his own hand, without a co-adjutor,
Novice, journey-man, or tutor.
Yet thus much I can give you as a token
Of his play's worth, no eggs are broken,
Nor quaking custards with fierce teeth affrighted
Wherewith your rout are so delighted;
Nor hales he in a gull, old ends reciting,
To stop gaps in his loose writing:
With such a deal of monstrous and forced action,
As might make Bethlem a faction:
Nor made he his play for jests stolen from each table,
But makes jests to fit his fable;
And so presents quick comedy, refined,
As best critics have designed;
The laws of time, place, persons he observeth,
From no needful rule he swerveth.

All gall and copperas from his ink he draineth,
Only a little salt remaineth,
Wherewith he'll rub your cheeks, till red, with laughter
They shall look fresh a week after.

BEN JONSON

(*b*)

Of those few fools, who with ill stars are curst,
Sure scribbling fools, call'd poets, fare the worst:
For they're a sort of fools which Fortune makes,
And after she has made 'em fools, forsakes.
With Nature's oafs 'tis quite a diff'rent case,
For fortune favours all her idiot-race.
In her own nest the cuckoo-eggs we find,
O'er which she broods to hatch the changeling-kind.
No portion for her own she has to spare.
So much she dotes on her adopted care.
Poets are bubbles, by the town drawn in,
Suffer'd at first some trifling stakes to win:
But what unequal hazards do they run!
Each time they write they venture all they've won:
The squire that's butter'd still, is sure to be undone.
This author, heretofore, has found your favour,
But pleads no merit from his past behaviour;
To build on that might prove a vain presumption,
Should grants to poets made admit resumption:
And in Parnassus he must lose his seat,
If that be found a forfeited estate.
He owns, with toil he wrought the following scenes,
But if they're naught, ne'er spare him for his pains:
Damn him the more; have no commiseration
For dullness on mature deliberation.
He swears he'll not resent one hiss'd-off scene,
Nor, like those peevish wits, his play maintain,
Who, to assert their sense, your taste arraign.
Some plot we think he has, and some new thought;
Some humour too; no farce, but that's a fault.

Satire, he thinks, you ought not to expect;
For so reform'd a town, who dares correct?
To please, this time, has been his sole pretence,
He'll not instruct, lest it should give offence.
Should he by chance a knave or fool expose,
That hurts none here, sure here are none of those.
In short, our play shall (with your leave to show it)
Give you one instance of a passive poet
Who to your judgements yields all resignation;
To save or damn, after your own discretion.

WILLIAM CONGREVE

These two verse prologues are addressed directly to the audience and introduce the plays which follow. The first is from Ben Jonson's *Volpone* (1606), the second from William Congreve's *The Way of the World* (1700). These two authors belong to totally different worlds. Can you detect this in the two prologues? They are both 'apologies' to the audience, which try to forestall criticism and give the audience a general idea of what to expect, as well as flattering it for its discrimination. Try to compare Jonson's 'frame of reference' with Congreve's.

Appendix A *A List of Suggestions for Further Reading*

This appendix suggests works that may be read at some time and covers fairly fully the kind of material that is discussed elsewhere in this book. Candidates for open scholarships in English may find this list of use as a basis for their reading, and others may make selections from the list to follow up particular interests. The list does not claim to be comprehensive, though anyone who had completed it would be very well-read.

(1) Poetry and Drama

CHAUCER:	*The Prologue* and one other tale (*Nonnes Preestes, Pardoners*).
SHAKESPEARE:	The four great tragedies (*King Lear, Macbeth, Othello, Antony and Cleopatra*); *Hamlet*; one of the comedies (*A Midsummer Night's Dream* or *Much Ado* or *Twelfth Night*); *Measure for Measure*; and either *The Tempest* or *The Winter's Tale*; a selection of the sonnets.
JONSON:	*The Alchemist, Volpone.*
MARLOWE:	*Dr Faustus.*
DONNE:	*Songs and Sonets*; *Elegies*; some of the *Divine Poems.*
GEORGE HERBERT:	A selection.
MARVELL:	*To His Coy Mistress*; *The Garden*; *Horatian Ode.*
MILTON:	Shorter Poems; *Paradise Lost, Books I and II.*
POPE:	*The Rape of the Lock*; *Moral Essays*; *An Epistle to Dr Arbuthnot.*
GOLDSMITH:	*The Deserted Village.*
JOHNSON:	*The Vanity of Human Wishes.*

WORDSWORTH:	*Lyrical Ballads*; the 'Lucy' poems; *Michael*; *The Prelude* (1805) Books I and II; a selection of the Sonnets.
COLERIDGE:	*The Ancient Mariner*; *Kubla Khan*; *Christabel*.
KEATS:	The five 'great' odes; *The Eve of St Agnes*; sonnets.
BYRON:	*The Vision of Judgement*; a selection of *Don Juan*.
ARNOLD:	*The Scholar Gipsy*; *Rugby Chapel*; *To Marguerite*, I and II.
MEREDITH:	*Modern Love*.
HOPKINS, ELIOT, D. H. LAWRENCE, YEATS, GRAVES, EDWARD THOMAS	Selections.

Selections from early anonymous and Elizabethan lyrics (there are many anthologies); and from *The Common Muse, ed.* de Sola Pinto, and *The Idiom of the People, ed.* James Reeves.

(2) NOVELS

FIELDING:	*Joseph Andrews*.
JANE AUSTEN:	*Pride and Prejudice*; *Mansfield Park*; *Emma*.
DICKENS:	*David Copperfield*; *Great Expectations*; *Hard Times*.
EMILY BRONTË:	*Wuthering Heights*.
CHARLOTTE BRONTË:	*Jane Eyre*; *Villette*.
GEORGE ELIOT:	*Silas Marner*; *Middlemarch*.
HARDY:	*The Trumpet Major*; *The Return of the Native*; *The Mayor of Casterbridge*.

CONRAD:	*Youth; The Nigger of the 'Narcissus'; The Heart of Darkness; Nostromo.*
D. H. LAWRENCE:	*Sons and Lovers; The Rainbow; Women in Love;* some short stories.
VIRGINIA WOOLF:	*To the Lighthouse.*
E. M. FORSTER:	*Howard's End; A Passage to India.*
JAMES JOYCE:	*Dubliners; Portrait of the Artist as a Young Man.*
KATHERINE MANSFIELD:	*The Garden Party* and other stories.

(3) OTHER PROSE

BUNYAN:	*The Pilgrim's Progress.*
SWIFT:	*Gulliver's Travels* (especially Book IV).
KEATS:	Letters, a selection.
ARNOLD:	*Culture and Anarchy.*
D. H. LAWRENCE:	Essays, travel books, letters.

Appendix B — *Some Critical and Related Books*

JOHNSON:	*Preface to Shakespeare;* parts of *Lives of the Poets.*
COLERIDGE:	Essays and lectures on Shakespeare, etc.
WORDSWORTH:	Preface to *Lyrical Ballads.*
ARNOLD:	Parts of *Essays in Criticism* esp. Second Series.
ELIOT:	*Selected Essays.*
F. R. LEAVIS:	*Revaluation;* parts of *New Bearings in English Poetry, The Common Pursuit, The Great Tradition.*
LESLIE STEPHEN:	*English Literature and Society in the Eighteenth Century.*
D. A. TRAVERSI:	*Approach to Shakespeare.*

L. C. KNIGHTS:	*Explorations*; *Some Shakespearean Themes*.
G. WILSON KNIGHT:	*The Wheel of Fire*; parts of other critical works.
EDMUND WILSON:	Parts of *Axel's Castle* and *The Wound and the Bow*.
WILLIAM EMPSON:	Parts of *Seven Types of Ambiguity* and *Some Versions of Pastoral*.
HENRI FLUCHÈRE:	*Shakespeare*.

NOTE 1. *The Pelican Guide to English Literature* ed. Boris Ford, in several volumes, is often useful and has admirable bibliographies for reference.

2. Two books of great general interest which do not fit into any of the above categories are Richard Hoggart's *The Uses of Literacy* and Raymond Williams' *Culture and Society*.